EVERLASTING LIFE

FROM THOUGHT TO REALITY

BEN AMMI

Published by **Communicators Press**
P.O. Box 26063, Washington, D.C. 20001
(202) 291-9244; FAX (202) 291-9149

ISBN 0-9620463-6-1

Library of Congress Catalog Card Number
94-071029

CREDITS

TABLE OF CONTENTS

FOREWORD i

A NOTE TO OUR READERS v

ABOUT THE AUTHOR vi

INTRODUCTION 1

'A PRAYER FOR UNDERSTANDING' 7

SPECIAL INTRODUCTORY
STUDY MATERIALS 11

    The Pathway to Faith 11

    Faith. . . And The Importance
    Of The Holy Language 15

    The Attributes
    That Lead To Faith 27

THE FAMINE 28

THE NEW (WORLD) ORDER 57

THE EVIL SPIRITS THAT
VIE FOR THE SOULS OF MEN 89

'THE GOOD SHIP JESUS' 101

THE SEEDS OF EVIL --
THE GRACE OF TRUTH 117

THE TRUTH ABOUT DEATH 129

THE GENESIS RESURRECTION 175

BIBLIOGRAPHY 189

FOREWORD

When I began to do research in preparation for writing the foreword to <u>Everlasting Life</u>, I came to the realization that the concept of everlasting life is commonly considered mythical or phenomenal. Living "forever", I realized, isn't a subject that's seriously considered by many people, even though ministers have preached the concept of everlasting life as long as there have been religions. However, every attempt I made to discuss the concept of everlasting life with people as a prelude to writing this foreword, was met with looks of concern for my sanity. No one today, in this world of incurable diseases like AIDS and leukemia, or wars and revolution, or plane, train and car crashes, escalating big city crime, and suicide, homicide, genocide, and patricide, considers that a life of 70 years is anything but normal. Yet, 6,000 years ago, when men were dependent on donkeys for transportation and an open fire for fuel, most people lived hundreds of years.

Most westerners are more preoccupied with death, than life. This is clearly evident when you turn on your television set or read any newspaper in the modern world. Have we seen so much war, violence, crime, hatred, perversion, and movies like "Death Becomes Her" until death is second nature to us now? News stories are overloaded with accounts about accidental death, murder (often broken down into degrees - first degree murder or second degree murder), suicide, manslaughter . . . the terms are endless. How is it that people have become so complacent and lackadaisical about death? Do we consider the death of siamese twin Amy Lakeberg trivial compared to the luscious details of her medical separation from her infant sister Angela? Was the replaying of Pamela Basu being dragged to her death by lowly carjackers typical dinner-time entertainment? Was the burning of the Branch Davidians' compound in Waco, Texas and the knowledge that whole families went up in smoke secondary to news that Janet Reno had "outmaneuvered" David Koresh? One must wonder if undertakers are the major stockholders in our nation's television and newspaper industries, because a dinner meal is just not palatable without an overabundance of death for dessert.

When did life become so meaningless until the name of the game became kill, do drugs, steal, lie, cheat, be promiscuous, 'cause "you gotta die some time, so live life to the fullest", as all the diehard cigarette smokers espouse. Despite people's daring behavior and "live and let die" attitude, don't most people expect to go to heaven to God who awaits us no matter what is done here on Earth? To assuage any guilt feelings, most people attend church, synagogue or mosque one day in the week, then the rest of the week "do their thing" be it cheating on their taxes, running a red light, imbibing two bottles of scotch a month, engaging in adulterous affairs, eating chemically-laden foods and using cancer-causing products in every aspect of their lives, with hardly a care, as though there's no tomorrow. You know, business as usual, believing that life is 70 or 80 years and that's it. Yet don't we all desire to live longer lives, to see our grandchildren's grandchildren? Has the ambition to find the fountain of youth culminated in the silicone injections and the cosmetic surgery?

The truth is, we all want to live long lives. Longevity has its attributes. We revere those who reach 100 years, celebrating long life as special. On one early morning television talk show each day, oldsters who have reached 100 years are featured. While meager praises are bestowed upon them, these elderly are actually looked upon as an aberration who have survived despite living in a world of torturous diseases, wars and rampant crime. We jokingly refer to them as being "old as Methuselah" (who lived 969 years). Yet, this is not expressed as a measure of reverence or as an optimistic display that we live equally as long. Naturally, nobody really believes anyone lived as long as 969 years. That's just another mythological tale found in the scriptures like Moses parting the Red Sea. It's certainly not talked about or hoped for. When my father brags that he's lived to be 82 years old, I remind him that the men of old lived centuries. He thinks I'm crazy, telling me that no one has ever lived that long.

Thus, it came as no surprise that my attempts to discuss everlasting life with the religious crowd were met with sighs of boredom and lack of seriousness. The concept of everlasting life has actually lost its verisimilitude and has become a catch phrase of the clergy like resurrection, or the Messiah: part of the vernacular of the religious trade. Yet as I delved into the pages of this new manuscript to critically approach an issue that I had no clear feelings about, I soon learned that death is not a part of life, and our Heavenly reward is not to die and go to God's outstretched arms. These images are false. We have been tricked to believe, by western religious leaders, scientists, health specialists, movie and television moguls and the media that death is ordinary and acceptable. It's perfectly all right to do anything, believe anything, and live recklessly. The idea of death bringing us closer to God is just a lie.

When did the lie about death and everlasting life get interwoven? When did we start believing in death more than life? What about the men of old who supposedly lived to be hundreds of years old? Did the writers of the Bible exaggerate? Did Adam really live to be 930 years old? And Seth 912? No one in recent history has lived much beyond 100 years. What has man done to bring on his own extinction, for surely if men of old lived 900 years and today we only live 70, something, somewhere has gone terribly wrong? With all the techno-logical advancements in science, medicine and social conditions, surely, we should be living longer lives, not shorter ones. Certainly if we can put a man on the moon, we can live to be 200 instead of 100. And if we can live to 200, why not 300, or 400?

To our knowledge no one has lived to recall the era of Napoleon, the Middle Passage, slavery or the Civil War? Everlasting life is a concept that few truly believe in because it has not been scientifically proven that anyone has ever lived "forever." Therefore, if the American Medical Association or any of the world's major universities have not acknowledged that life everlasting is a possibility, then no one believes in it. Yet if everlasting life was to be a myth or an anomaly, why has the concept hovered over us like the clouds in the sky: there, but not there?

It's time to take it seriously. In Everlasting Life, Ben Ammi warns that the time has come to obliterate the acceptance of death and supplant it with the Godly belief that life can be eternal if God's instructions are properly followed and adhered to. Death is not the first step on the road "Home" as funeral directors and ministers would have you believe. Furthermore, taking life for granted, living haphazardly and recklessly, is one of man's greatest sins.

Before you dismiss Everlasting Life as just another theological self-help book or an accusatory finger-pointing at all your sins and errors, consider the times in which we live and how desperately we need right answers. This is the fourth in a series of very profound and very serious teachings that have touched nearly a million lives and successfully opened minds to the plethora of lies and deceptions that have absolutely and inexorably blinded our society into accepting death as a God-sanctioned, common place event. Ben Ammi explains that death is not the norm and those who have accepted it as a part of life have done so ignorantly because when God created man, He planned on our lives being everlasting.

Many will find the writing on this subject implausible, incredible and too fantastic to believe. But there are those who have read Ben Ammi before, who have witnessed his truths come to the light and who know that his words rarely, if ever, fall to the ground.

Everlasting Life is our key to everlasting survival. The truth is Methuselah did live to be 969 and now, maybe, we can too.

Odehyah Baht Israel

iv

A Note To Our Readers

You will frequently encounter the use of the term "Euro-gentile" throughout this work. It is a term coined by the African Hebrew Israelites in keeping with our having seized the "Power to Define," a concept which was discussed in detail in the book, God The Black Man And Truth."

The suffix "gentile" simply denotes a people or nation that is without the knowledge of the True and Living God of Creation. When using the term "Euro-gentile," (often interchangeably with "Euro-American"), we are in fact referring to the entire European family of nations; i.e., Europe, the United States of America, Canada, South Africa, New Zealand, Australia, etc.

Its usage also reflects the pervasive and powerful social, economic, cultural and political influence these nations have wielded on this planet. As such, though these "Euro-gentile" nations are obviously and unquestionably responsible for having brought all of humanity and creation to the brink of destruction as a result of their continuously evil activities and deeds, no racist or otherwise negative connotations are inferred by the phrase.

You will also notice the capitalization of the word "black," when referring to race, as opposed to merely color. We are well aware that this usage may not conform to generally-accepted norms of the English language.

While the use of "Black" may thus be deemed inaccurate, it must be recognized that many "Blacks" or "Africans" have not yet arrived to the point of tracing and identifying their particular nation of origin, or nationality. It is an obvious fact that our skins are black and that "Black Americans" hail collectively from the continent of Africa.

Again, many other words and terms may be capitalized; e.g., "Truth," "Divine," "Love," or "Power to Define." When they appear in such formal usage, it denotes their application as a principle "building block" or concept in the New World Order.

About The Author

What does one make of Ben Ammi?

What does one make of a man who consistently confronts that which appears impossible and inconceivable. Then he transforms the impossibility... first, to something plausible and ultimately to something attainable.

After reading all of his books and comparing these writings with his work, I have come to the conclusion that it is not the obstacle that is being transformed by Ben Ammi's work. It is our minds. Let me explain.

There was nothing "obviously" unusual about his early years that would foretell the ability he would later exhibit. Ben Ammi was born in 1939, on the southwest side of Chicago. He went to Washburn Trade School, only to drop out. He finished his high school education during a stint in the U.S. army, serving at a local missile base. At the end of his tour of duty, he married and took a job at the Howard Foundry working as a metallurgist.

It was during this time that he met elder Eliyahoo Buie, Ben's first mentor of Hebrew history, who confirmed many things that Ben's parents had told him regarding the history of African people and the

Bible. The fruit of this inspiration lead Ben Ammi to co-found the Abeta Hebrew Cultural Center on Chicago's south side, which would serve as the platform for the exceptional intellect that would come forth from his writings and works.

Here is a man born and raised in inner city Chicago, with all of its known pitfalls. In 1966, at the "seasoned" age of 26, he had the audacity, charisma and conviction to inspire more than 350 African Americans to leave their families, friends and the only life they had ever known to journey into the unknown world of the African bush.

That he would survive Chicago is unlikely enough. But then to convince so many to join him on such an improbable journey is unthinkable. But he did. They went and they survived.

He did not have the reassuring benefits of having traveled that way before or being trained in the how-to's of life in the west African bush with its sweltering heat, driving rain and without any of the conveniences of modern life.

Their ultimate destination was Israel. That's right. Israel, a land none of them had ever seen and barely knew actually existed. Again, the inconceivable. But in 1969, they arrived in the Holy Land. Once there, they announced to the world that they had come to establish the long-awaited, prophesied Kingdom of God -- a society where the ills of modern society ceased to exist. A place where men and women in search of truth and a reconnection with God could begin to fashion a New World Order.

Impossible, you think? Certainly to the outside observer, this would prove to be the undoing of Ben Ammi and his followers. They settled in the Negev Desert in southern Israel, a region where more and more Israelis are finding it impossible to scratch out a respectable living. They were having what seemed to be one problem after another. Press reports said they were starving. The government was threatening to throw them out. They were criminals, the news reports said. All the while Ben Ammi, maintained that the community had struck upon the keys to life, and the establishment of the Kingdom of God on earth.

Community members took on some of the most entrenched problems of the day and progressed. They became noted for lack of crime, no drug abuse and the true strengthening of the family both nuclear and communal, at a time when all of these plagues were spiraling upward throughout the modern world.

In 1982, when he published God the Black Man and Truth, the first work in his "Resurrection Trilogy," it stood as a challenge to conventional thinking about our relationship to God, the role of the Black man in the process of redemption of all men, and the inescapable Truth of Almighty God.

Most critics overlooked the fact that the work was throughly rooted in the Holy Bible. They tried to pigeon-hole Ben Ammi into one of the existing frameworks for literature done by angry Black men who came of political age in the 1960's. That he was clearly unique became more evident in his writings to come.

With the publication of God and the Law of Relativity, in 1991, we saw another side of Ben Ammi. Still, emersed in the Holy Bible, he wrote about the simple affairs of everyday life and the indisputable laws of nature which dictate the response of our every deed. The writings were easy to understand, yet extraordinarily profound.

And it was about this same time that we saw another side of the incredible community which had developed from the obscure beginnings of more than two decades prior. A diplomatic breakthrough had taken place and the community in Dimona was being received and exposed at another level. Increasing numbers of visitors from all over the world came and bore witness to the highly structured, series of institutions established. People were living free of crime, drugs and vice. A vegan community reaching new heights of creativity in diet / nutrition and exercise, family structure, organic agriculture and sharing.

Then came the third and most challenging installment of the Trilogy, "The Messiah and the End of This World." I guess by now, anyone familiar with the writings or works of Ben Ammi, should not have been surprised that he was targeting some of the most disputed and emotionally charged issues of the spiritual and religious institutions of the day such as the recognition of the Messiah, the anti-Christ, the 666 and more.

Readers of the "Resurrection Trilogy," have been exposed to an entirely new way, even a new world of thinking. It was a world that existed not merely in print or in theory, but the fruits of which were the motivation for the accomplishments of the Hebrew Israelite Community, which Ben Ammi continued to serve as spiritual leader.

He was much more than an author. He had taken on some of the most challenging subjects and re-cast them in simple terms, all relating to God and the Holy Bible. The positions he espoused called for the discussion of the Bible and humanity's relationship to it in a non-emotional manner and in the light of new possibilities.

Which brings us to 1994 and this, Ben Ammi's fourth book entitled, Everlasting Life. Perhaps by now we should expect the unexpected. Whether we are prepared to take a serious look at the prospect of life everlasting or not, we are bound by his record of success to read the words of Ben Ammi with another mind.

Everlasting Life, is a work far beyond the mechanics of diet, exercise or the latest medical technological breakthrough. It is Ben Ammi's continued challenge to us all, to fully believe and live the Word which many of us have professed to love.

Truly the thought of living forever has taunted humanity and spiced folklore throughout history. Yet, in this modern world, the attaining of everlasting life was less the domain of the God who created man -- but likely the scientific possibility granted by a highly technically indoctrinated man.

Ben Ammi, has brought us and the pursuit of everlasting life, back to God Almighty and His infinite wisdom, in terms comprehendible and deeds which are possible.

Upon reading Everlasting Life, you are sure to experience a new thought... which leads to a new reality.

Prince Immanuel Ben Yehuda

INTRODUCTION

In this writing I've been moved by the Holy Spirit to pave before you a clear path to life eternal so that no man can plead ignorance if the wrong choice is made. The Holy One of Israel has blessed me with the necessary intellect that I may shine His light (intelligence) upon you and unravel the hidden mystery about life, that it may once again be pursued; and that death be defeated. In order to overcome death, you must make the courageous choice of rejecting many of the institutionalized teachings and doctrines that are now proliferated and see them as being responsible for much of the world's spiritual and physical degeneracy. My heart is heavy as no doubt was Yeshua's as he watched Nicodemus walk away after his world - rotating upon the axis of a lie - was exposed.

"And for this cause God shall send them strong delusion, that they should believe a lie:

That they all might be damned who believed not the truth, but had pleasure in unrighteousness."

II Thessalonians 2:11-12

1

I begin this work with a comprehensive discourse on Faith. In this chapter I pry open the hidden understanding by following the development of the three Hebrew consonants that form the root of the word Faith. You need not know or speak any Hebrew to comprehend the lesson. Faith is essential, for it alone will provide the substance of things you hope for. If you are to ever know the truth of my words, or to reap the fruit (reward), it can only be achieved by initial faith in the seed (source). If you have faith and plant this seed in your mind, your works will provide the necessary substance to pursue and acquire the eternal life of the harvest.

My exegesis on life eternal is the truth brought and revealed unto me by the Holy Spirit, as an essential element of the gospel of the Kingdom of God. It is not medical, scientific or technological, for I've scribed eternal life in another realm, another world, a world of Truth. To enjoy the benefits of these words, you will have to be born again into this world of truth. The objective of truth is to challenge and overcome the trappings of this present world system. To accomplish this feat, it must be exposed to intensive truth. Thus it can be judged and relinquished of its authority over the human family.

There is what I term an anti-life mentality which has been/is being disseminated by the anti-life force on this earth. The tyrant, the anti-life force has been deeply implanted in your mind. The classroom is its formative laboratory; your outer environment substitutes when class is adjourned. This force has succeeded in processing the lie into your cells, tissues and organs.

Once you are convinced that sickness and death are normal, you then anticipate sickness; whereby you prepare to die. However, in order for you to wage a successful war against sickness and death, you will have to be convinced that they are not normal. It is a formidable challenge to reprogram a mind to life that has been programmed to die. Out of all of God's pre-eminent creatures within His Holy Creation, it is man only that has lost his way. His perceptions, concepts, beliefs and understanding of God have been debased lower than the least of God's creations. He alone within this grand universal order has attempted to change, alter and improve the perfection of God. Therefore he is bound and trapped in a web of falsehood, untruths and lies. Man's life nevertheless is similar to that of all of God's creatures and creations. The criterion for becoming eligible to receive everlasting life is the same - remain within the universal cycles of righteousness.

> *The fruit of the righteous is a tree of life; and he that winneth souls is wise.*

> **Proverbs 11:30**

> *In the way of righteousness is life, and in the pathway thereof there is no death.*

> **Proverbs 12:28**

Throughout the pages of this book it is my objective to open the eyes of the blind and the ears of the deaf to the words of Truth. My emphasis is placed upon the God element, not the god of religion, but that all powerful, conquering universal force - the God of Life. When you turned aside from the God of the original creation, you deviantly regressed into the realm of an entirely different creature and environment, in both mind and body. You developed new, negative thought patterns, beliefs and emotions that subsequently created chemical reactions that negatively affect every cell in your body. The contemporary mindsets, beliefs, inappropriate objectives and goals effectively prevent the true life experience from entering your realm.

In retrospection, I recall a conversation between myself and an avid non-believer in the laws of God. I inquired: Do you feel that because you do not believe in the laws of God, they cease to govern you and determine your blessings and/or curses?

He replied in the affirmative. We continued our dialogue. Further, "Would you agree that this universe and all of its creations and creatures are governed by law and order?" "Well, that is with the exception of 'man'", according to your initial reply. Perhaps your comprehension would become more vivid if I defined blessings and curses in a more simple and less archaic or supernatural terminology. Blessings and curses are not strokes of luck - good or bad. Blessings are the reward for abiding by the Universal Laws. Curses are simply the absolute result of violating them. A simple example: After monitoring the lifespan very closely of drinkers of alcoholic beverages and smokers, would you label those who indulged and did not contract a cancer or other type of malady blessed, and those that did cursed? The Truth of the matter is that those that were not affected by the diseases were certainly not blessed, but lucky. You see, lungs were created to perform harmoniously within this grand universal order to breathe air - pure air. Otherwise they will, generally speaking, malfunction. The non-smoker or drinkers that do not believe in God and Truth principally are more likely to maintain healthier lungs and livers than their counterparts. That is their luck, not blessing. But we may be assured that nonetheless, their minds are concentrating on the destruction of some other organ or tissue like the heart, or colon, pressing their luck in a life of uncertainty. Good health is the result of a righteous lifestyle within a suitable environment.

I've stressed in this work that intelligence is creative. Everything you now think and feel emotionally reflects who you are or who you will be. Wrong intelligence will/can create an evil being whose mind is obligated to create an evil environment. That force of intelligence understandably has the power to define life and death; wealth and poverty; youthfulness, as well as old age. Because his spiritual intelligence is limited, his world is of limited existence. My heart is very heavy for all those that believe sickness and death are unavoidable; over the hill at forty; old at fifty, senile and sedentary at sixty, and facing death at seventy. Unknowingly, you have simply been programmed by an anti-life (anti-God) spirit to prevent your natural rebellion against prevarication. In the final analysis, you lose your youth simply because you don't know how to preserve it. Once you are rendered helpless in the so-called accredited institutions, the confiscation of the values of life is relatively easy.

In addition, we must broaden the scope of our struggle against the anti-life force and confront it from an international/universal aspect. The forces of err continuously instill the subtle impression that each person should be personally satisfied with setting his/herself in order, as if we are a disconnected, individualistic self-contained entity. We all certainly can recall the very rude awakening to passive smoking (the effects of the inhaled smoke of a smoker on an non-smoker). The

4

individual that abstains from smoking or that struggles and finally overcomes that lustful, deadly habit suddenly realizes that he can still fall victim to lung cancer if he's in an environment with others that smoke. Otherwise, in order to create a safe haven upon this planet, we must not be independent and possess the "every man for himself" mentality, which now governs the world's masses.

The struggle for my life engulfs the entire cosmos. We can't give the anti-life force one safe haven on this planet. We must have an environment/world of friends, relatives, associates whose lifestyles are conducive to proper or correct life aspirations. I am very serious about not becoming a victim of sickness; therefore I must not allow others to destroy my health. We are all affected by the things taking place around us. Subsequently, we must endeavor to be certain that the right things are transpiring within our environment.

The Holy One of Israel has also blessed me to take you on a sacred journey into the realm of the Holy Spirit. It is the principal reason that the Bible, as an indispensable tool of liberation, has to be reassessed in the light of ancient truth instead of contemporary deception. As we return to Biblical truth and away from contemporary religion, we will find the essential fundamental understanding of the Holy Spirit as revealed in these writings to be Truth.

The understanding of the Holy Spirit is a prerequisite for activation of the armies of heaven. These armies represent the active force that has been/shall be placed under the direct command of the anointed of God. One has to be very circumspect in calling upon spirits, for there is no room for error. Evil spirits are also actively supporting the forces of evil. If someone calls upon a spirit that is active on behalf of satan, there is a strong possibility that all the works of his hands shall be destroyed and neither shall his name ever be inscribed in the Book of Life.

Linguistically, I've again substituted the correct "Yeshua," (instead of "Jesus") the name of the carpenter from Nazareth, son of Joseph and Mary. Initially you may find it somewhat awkward to adjust, but if you overcome the initial sensitivity and fear, you will find that new horizons of strength and understanding will be your reward. As I look back at the historical parallels, I am reminded by the wisdom of the ancient inspired prophets of God that the sins of a people or an individual can become so numerous and complex that their only hope becomes a new beginning or a new birth. So it is with the human family. You've been inundated with far too many lies to sort through one by one. The words that have been recorded on these pages are for all that will believe them and do them - a new beginning, the choice of a lifetime.

I've also included in my dissertation on Everlasting Life, an in-depth review and explanation of the Genesis resurrection. Much of the contemporary concepts of resurrection of the dead were born out of folklore, mythology and legends, later incorporated into religious concepts and beliefs by various nations upon the planet earth. They are incongruous with the original message that was conveyed by the Holy Spirit. For example, there is an Indian belief that it is forbidden to kill insects because human beings are resurrected through them in various stages of spiritual elevation. Christians perceive the hereafter (opening of the literal graveyards and the righteous resurrected to paradise and the wicked into hellfire.)

Likewise, the Islamic concept of the resurrection is that the righteous and wrong deeds of man will be weighed on the scale of justice which will determine his fate after death: Heaven (paradise) or hell. However, from the Hebraic perspective, three forms of resurrection exist. First is תחיה (ti-kee-yah), a quickening or revival (mental) of God's spirit. The essence of the renovation where one becomes conscious of Truth, acknowledging God and fulfilling His will. Second is קימה (ke-mah) to establish oneself; to rise to one's feet. The spiritually inert spring up and into action for God, activated by the Holy Spirit. Third is הקצה (ha-kaht-sah) - a dreadful, fearful awakening (seeing or being made aware of the loss of one's soul to the underworld).

Actually, the true resurrection is really the day of triumph for the Word of God; the day when God's word (Truth) will suddenly come alive and install in men the desire to live again under the simple rulership of God.

"A Special Prayer for Understanding from Jerusalem"

"And he spoke a parable unto them to this end, that men ought always to pray, and not to faint."

Luke 18:1

One of the oddities of the times when Yeshua of Nazareth was preaching at Jerusalem, was that the people had forgotten how to pray. One of the peculiarities of these times is that African Americans have forgotten how to pray.

"And it came to pass that, as he was praying in a certain place, when he ceased, one of his disciples said unto him, Lord, teach us to pray, as John also taught his disciples."

Luke 11:1

"If they sin against thee (for there is no man who sinneth not), and thou be angry with them, and deliver them to the enemy, so that they carry them away captives unto the land of the enemy, far or near;

Yet if they shall take it to their hearts in the land where they were

7

carried captives, and repent, and make supplication unto thee in the land of them who carried them captives, saying we have sinned and have done perversely, we have committed wickedness;

And so return unto thee with all their hearts and with all their soul, in the land of their enemies, who led them away captive, and pray unto thee toward their land, which thou gavest unto their fathers, the city which thou has chosen, and the house which I have built for thy name.

Then hear thou their prayer and their supplication in heaven, thy dwelling place, and maintain their cause."

I Kings 8:46-49

"And the Lord said unto him, I have heard thy prayer and thy supplication, that thou hast made before me; I have hallowed this house, which thou hast built, to put my name there forever; and mine eyes and mine heart shall be there perpetually."

I Kings 9:3

"A Prayer For Understanding"

Lord God of Israel, there is no God like unto Thee in Heaven above or on earth beneath for Thou keepeth covenant and mercy with Thy servants that walk before Thee with all their heart. I beseech Thee, have respect unto the prayer and to the supplication of thy servant, O Lord my God, to hearken unto the cry and the prayer which thy servant doth pray before Thee this day. And hearken Thou to the supplication of Thy people, and hear Thou in Heaven Thy dwelling place, and when Thou hear, forgive; then teach them the good way wherein they should walk and be not angry with them but deliver them from the hands of the adversary, for they be Thy people and Thy inheritance which Thou brought forth out of Egypt from the midst of the iron furnace.

Lord God be with us as Thou was with our fathers; leave us not; neither forsake us. Incline our hearts unto Thee to walk in all Thy ways and to keep Thy commandments, Thy statutes and Thy judgements. And let these my words wherewith I have made supplication before the Lord, be nigh unto Thee day and night that You maintain the cause of Thy servant and the cause of Thy people Israel at all times as the matter shall require, that all the people of the earth may know that Thou art God and there is none else.

Father, Thy people are destroyed for lack of knowledge; we have rejected the instructions of God, therefore our enemies rule over us. Our glory has been turned into shame; our young men fall in the streets; we weep for our children and they are not. The daughters of Zion have been consumed by the adversary; the sons of Judah no longer provide a defense. Thy standard bearers have fallen. The enemy has come up very high, and we have sunk very low. We sought the ways of the adversary and only increased our sorrow. We have eaten of the tree of which Thou said, Ye shall not eat of it lest ye die. Father, in our sorrow we cry unto Thee for we know not the way, but Thou knowest; we understand not, but Thou understandeth; we see not, but Thou seest. Teach us good judgment and knowledge; make us to understand the way of Thy precepts, for it is time to work for God.

This I recall to my mind; therefore have I hope. It is of the Lord's mercies that we are not consumed because His compassions fail not. All that pass by clap their hands; they hiss and wag their head at the daughter of Thy people, saying: Is this the people that men call the perfection of beauty: The joy of the whole earth? All mine enemies have opened their mouths against me. They hiss and gnash their teeth; they say we have swallowed her up! Certainly this is the day that we looked for. We have found; we have seen it. O Father, we have been thrown down; they have not pitied; the enemy rejoiced over us. Oh Lord God of Israel, hear, for the Lord will not cast off forever. Send Thy spirit into me like the lightning from the heavens. Open my eyes that I may see Thy light on the path; open mine ears that I may hear Thy words and follow Thy instructions. We seek Thee O Father, for in Thee only is our salvation. We seek Thy way, for in it there is life. Remember O Lord what is come upon us; consider and behold our reproach. Our inheritance is turned to strangers; our houses to aliens. Our necks are under persecution; we labor and have no rest. Our fathers have sinned and are not, and we have borne their iniquity. Servants have ruled over us, thinking there is none to deliver out of their hand. But Thy wisdom shall deliver us; Thy knowledge shall restore our glory; Thy understanding, our greatness. Thou shall restore our soul and once again cause us to lie down in green pastures. We are Thy children; Thou art our Father. Be one again with Thy servant. For we are the sheep of Thy pasture; the work of Thine hands. Forsake us not at this the fateful hour.

Selah.

SPECIAL INTRODUCTORY STUDY MATERIALS

The Pathway to Faith

"My son, if thou wilt receive my words, and lay my commandments with thee,

So that thou incline thine ear unto wisdom, and apply thine heart to understanding;

Yea if thou criest after knowledge, and liftest up thy voice for understanding;

If thou seekest her as silver, and searches for her as for hidden treasures;

Then shalt thou understand the fear of the Lord, and find the knowledge of God.

Proverbs 2:1-5

Many great things have been forwarded to us by the prophets of God by way of the Bible. We are therefore obligated to be diligent and skillful in order to unlock its hidden treasures. While having access to various translations of the Bible, we are admonished to pay particular respect and attention to the original version - the Hebrew. Other translations vary widely and often lack the original intensity and root meaning of the words and passages from which they are derived.

With the exception of a few chapters in the Book of Daniel, the entire Bible is written in the Holy tongue, Hebrew. Hebrew was spoken by all of the great men of the Bible such as Moses, Abraham, the inspired prophets of Israel and Yeshua of Nazareth.

Contrary to popular misconceptions held today, the words and instructions of the prophets were not vague, ambiguous, inapplicable and therefore ineffective interpretations of the word of God. The prophets communicated the true understanding of its content and meaning - full of relevance and practical application to our continuing struggle for Truth, righteousness and justice.

The lesson in this writing is the timeless essence of the wisdom, knowledge and understanding intended to heal the soul of man. These teachings are the "Keys to Life" under a government of men governed by God. They will help you to avoid many problems in your day-to-day life, as you start the journey back to a harmonious relationship with God. You will draw closer to God, because you applied His instructions according to the charge given by His messengers.

If you apply the wisdom taught in these pages, you will be able to help your friends, relatives and neighbors through stressful situations. You will be able to make their lives more rewarding by sharing with them the plan of salvation and strengthening their relationship with the Eternal God of Creation.

There were many things heard and repeated throughout our childhood that were never really understood. Terms that no one seemed capable or dared give a clear comprehendable explanation. One such term is "FAITH". The connotations of faith seemed to always indicate something to do with God and the Bible. To hear someone say he had faith could mean that he was in close harmony with God. To be referred to as "one of little faith" could be frightening.

But now the night is far spent, as evidenced by the separation of church and state, religion and righteousness. The obligation of governments to instill the teachings of Godliness and the fear of God amongst the people does not exist in modern society. The line between good and evil has been blurred. Howbeit, faith is being taught daily in Euro-gentile institutions - it is a strange "faith" that is in opposition to God.

> *"And no marvel; for Satan himself is transformed into an angel of light.*
>
> *Therefore it is no great thing if his ministers also be transformed as the ministers of righteousness; whose end shall be according to their works."*
>
> **II Corinthians 11:14-15**

This is a scientifically advanced age. Yet this world is beset with problems on every side, problems that the governments cannot solve, or problems that they do not desire to solve. Why are so many evils that threaten man's safety and security *allowed to flourish* as if out of control? Could it be the problem is "Faith"? What is the connection between faith and nationality, if any? Unquestionably, my brethren, faith is certainly not a subject relegated solely to one's religious teachings. This fundamental belief has been very misleading and subtly deceptive. It has been the objective of the Euro-gentile statesman to convince the layman that the influence of God (or satan) is mainly perpetrated through religious institutions (not so much the normal educational institutions). This is how the statesmen deceived the populace into believing that church and state, or God and the government, could be separated. In reality such a separation is neither practical nor possible.

Purposefully, faith was alluded to as a religious term by the early advocates of Euro-gentile theology. It seems that European religion, for some reason, is at the heart of many deep misconceptions that have led humanity away from God. It seems to have had the effect of anesthesia, putting the mind into a deep coma-like sleep, while allowing the politicians a freehand in leading the masses into the waiting arms of satan. I have concluded that there is something grossly wrong - spiritually, morally and truthfully - with contemporary religion. It seems to be part and parcel of a diabolical universal plot to destroy the true God-presence from among men.

Surely this position will make some of you uncomfortable. But remember the role of religion in the deception of the masses, is not a new phenomenon. Just as in the days of Yeshua the misinformation promulgated by the church was at the core of the problems of the society. To overcome this, there has to be a return to the fundamental (pre-European) concepts concerning spirituality, the human family and truth.

Every government upon this earth is under the influence of God or satan; by their fruit we shall know them. We can certainly testify to the relative ease with which you can find killers, bandits, robbers, pimps, liars, thieves, exploiters, drug lords, homosexuals, pedophiliacs, sadistic torturers of the innocent and haters of God. The production lines that are turning out evil are abundant and efficient. However, men of God are a very scarce commodity, and most of the human family are too destroyed by religion and mis-education to reverse the trend.

The world's inhabitants have been made exceptionally strong in their faith in the adversary of God, the devil. This did not occur merely as a result of the one-day-a-week visit to the local religious institution. The far greater damage was done in the institutions of learning under the influence of err. How else could the devil have deceived the WHOLE WORLD?

> *"People have reached the conclusion that the more educated a society becomes, the more that society can advance in the world. In reality, the more a society advances in **mis-education**, the more that society loses the relationship between cause and effect. The more educated any society becomes, the more its citizens believe that they and their nation can act with complete impunity."*

> *"We would like to re-emphasize the fact that everything in the human world is completely backwards. If the human idea is that something like religion or education is divinely inspired, it is more likely to be a product*

of the worse kind of human darkness. There will be many, many years before humanity can comprehend this reality."

Modern Education: One Size Fits All
Mary E. Carreiro

One thing you must bear in mind as you study: you must hear the Word of the Lord. How do you know when someone hears? By our works we prove that we have or have not heard. Men are taught to drive automobiles, to solve mathematical problems, to sow and to reap. Men must also be taught how to have faith in God. The development of the divine attribute of faith begins with hearing. If we cannot hear, we are not able to receive the formula for faith. The formula to which we refer passes through the ears enroute to your mind. It will teach you to think, to discern between good and evil, to make proper decisions, to govern your soul... to live. Men today no longer know how to think; they have lost their (God) minds.

For example, men invented and built nuclear arsenals because they sought to protect themselves, from each other. Now they have weapons not to protect themselves, but to destroy themselves. They are now trying to protect themselves from being destroyed by the weapons they built for their protection!

Men possessed by a strange spirit, not knowing how to think, have built large condominiums, wherein one can live with very little need to journey outside into the environment. They have "fun" by drinking alcoholic beverages, smoking cigarettes, eating caviar, because they no longer know how to discern or make proper decisions to govern their souls. . . to live.

Faith. . . And
The Importance Of The Holy Language

In this writing we are investigating a word we hear frequently... Faith. What did/does it mean in Hebrew? What is its significance? The Holy Tongue alone can reveal the in-depth meaning of this word and message of the Scribes of God. For this reason, the study of the

Holy Language is very important. When studying Hebrew from the root consonants, one is able to obtain a more precise understanding of the message, not just the word, by following their continuity in the family of words. This expanded understanding - "the Hebrew thought" - delves far beyond the definitions and connotations found in any other language. The great danger and potential that exists for misinterpretation becomes explicitly clear, upon fully comprehending the depth of "the Hebrew thought".

As we explore this subject, be very attentive to the Hebrew letter illustrations. These visual aids will assist you in understanding the prophetic message with relative ease. The enlarged root letters *alef, mem, noon**, (א-מ-ן) appear consistently, that you may follow the continuity of the relationship between the various subject words. You must follow these root letters for you will find them in every word discussed hereafter (with the exception of one), as we show the relativity of each word to faith. The definitions given are from the precise Hebrew translated into English.

Let us find FAITH. . .

אמונה - (Eh-moo-nah), formed from the root Hebrew letters אמן (alef, mem, noon) means faith.

לאמן - (Le-Ah-Main), in Hebrew means *to confirm, verify your belief; to educate; to train,* or we could truthfully say, *to begin the process of attaining faith.* Let us make an in-depth investigation of one of the meanings mentioned above. . . confirm. Again, in the infinitive form. . .

לאמן - (Le-Ah-Main) *to confirm: to make firm or firmer; to strengthen; to give new assurance of the validity; to remove doubt by authoritative act or indisputable fact.* If you hear, then you must confirm what you hear. A person confirms or strengthens what he hears through learning. He is able to be educated in what he has heard by attending classes and participating in every learning situation possible.

*ן/נ - *there are two forms of the noon.*

16

For example, the best guitarist in the country has begun a guitar class and you have been wanting to learn to play a guitar. *If you heard,* then you would verify this by allowing him to train you. You will learn to play by following instructions; you will be prompt in attending classes, and give yourself to his guidance. You will allow him to educate you. And if you really hear, every time you go to his class, you will confirm your belief; strengthen your belief; verify your belief. You confirm by your actions that you believe what you heard in the beginning regarding his ability to play the guitar.

Next we have. . .

אֵימוּן - (E-Moon) *training, practice; confirmation.* In simple terms, doing what you have been taught to do. If there is no practice, then there is no faith! If you practice what you have been taught, then you move on higher. You will find excellence, and will show forth diligence and discipline. You are learning to love (your/the guitar) and preparing to share, which brings us to...

לְהַאֲמִין - (Le-Hah-Ah-Me-N) *to believe; to trust by causing others to believe.* If you do not confirm your faith through your deeds, then you are not able to prove your belief while causing others to believe. You teach others to believe in your instructor while you confirm your belief through your actions. You are teaching and learning at the same time. Teaching in Hebrew is derived from the same word for learning. In other words, teaching is "intensified learning." That is to say, that one has to study diligently to become a teacher, and even more so to remain one. You teach others to believe in your teacher and at the same time you are rewarded by a strengthening of your own affirmation. Giving honor to a great man increases your respect. Do not be egocentric. For the greater your teacher, the greater you become. You are seen through the greatness of your teacher. Once convinced that you were trained by a great scholar, the people will desire to be taught by you, feeling that through you, they too may share in his greatness. Do not make your teacher seem small, for in doing so you belittle yourself.

At the next level we find...

נֶאֱמָן - (Neh-Eh-Mah-N) *faithful, trustworthy; reliable.* When the student becomes faithful, the teacher can have confidence in him. He can put a degree of trust in him. The individual is now ready for a level of responsibility. He can be numbered with those upon whom you rely. He will become more active in the building process. His energies are placed at your disposal. He is declaring his allegiance to a person, movement or a cause. His education can be expanded. You will find yourself giving more of your time and self unto him. We cite an example. During the early years of slavery in the United States, the African slave was constantly watched, monitored and trained, while being shaped and molded into a "negro". It was only after the master was reasonably confident of his reliability that he began to further the educational process, slowly expanding his learning at a level commensurate to his trust and dependability.

The very same process and tactics were employed by the Euro-gentile nations in their rape and plunder of the world. Through colonization, alien traditions and institutions were established throughout Africa and the "under-developed world," the great majority of which still stand to this day. Shortly thereafter, the Euro-gentile institutions of higher learning flung open their gates, ready to continue the process of training unwitting souls in the furtherance of their own destruction. Those that master the prescribed course are found trustworthy, reliable and faithful to the cause of Paris, London, Washington, etc. Every African should be extremely suspect and careful of European education, except in pursuit of training under direction of his government. Except that one is circumspect, the end result will be great faith in Europe, with no faith in Africa, and the devotion of one's energies to maintain European society, instead of helping to build one's own.

The next level. . .

אוֹמָן or אוֹמִין - (Oh-Mah-N or Oo-Mah-N) *trainer, educator; craftsman; artisan; master.* I must surely remind you that we're on the pathway to dismantling the very deceptive religious connotation of faith. The previously mentioned aspects of faith have very little to do with teachings on "faith" that you received during your Sunday visits to church. These new aspects of faith bring into focus your entire way of life and livelihood, and how you must sustain yourself by using the talents attained.

At this stage of your journey, you can begin to see the role of the educational institution in which you were awarded a "certificate of approval" deeming you worthy to apply your skills in building or perpetuating society's objectives. The statement: "You must attain higher education to succeed," becomes clear, as well as the relationship of trustworthiness to the level of education. That is to say, one with little education (training) is more likely not to be trusted.

In every country on earth the underclass is the most vilified of the society. Why? Because they cannot be relied upon nor trusted at the faithful hour. They are regarded as a threat by the earth's rulers. They rebel at the drop of a hat; they have no faith in politics. They are prey to all. Everything evil seems to find them and flourish in their midst. In comparison, the society's trust in you - and your faith in it - is measured by what you attain in your training.

Every Saint of God has to be a master, trainer or craftsman of some sort. No one dedicated unto God can continuously be taught, yet never learn. The Sons and Daughters of God at this juncture in history, must master the God way. Hence, the possession of each of God's talents becomes an affirmation of faith in God.

Therefore, when questioned concerning your talents, if the response is always negative- "I can build a little, cook a little, sew a little, expound a little and understand a little," then it stands to reason that, you've listened a little, had little training (attending classes), little have you caused others to believe, be relied upon very little, can't be trusted but a little and. . . have very little faith in God and His kingdom. Evil will attach itself unto you and flourish in your midst. Yeshua said, "O ye of little faith." He could easily find them (the faithless) because they were always sinking or drowning.

"And the Lord came down to see the city and the tower, which the children of men builded.

And the Lord said, Behold, the people are one, and they have all one language; and this they begin to do: and now nothing will be withheld from them, which they have imagined to do.

Come, let us go down, and there confound their language, that they may not understand one another's speech.

So the Lord scattered them abroad from there upon the face of all the earth: and they ceased building the city.

Therefore is the name of it called Babel, because the Lord did there confound the language of all the earth: and from there did the Lord scatter them abroad upon the face of all the earth. "

Genesis 11:5-9

There was a time after the creation when all men spoke the same tongue. In that one language they were considered one nation under God with the power to do all that they could imagine. Had their imaginations been to do what was good in the sight of God, unbridled power would have been at their disposal. Yet under the influence of the Spirit of err (satan), men imagined to compete with, instead of serve, God. Consequently, God thought to weaken and confuse men. To accomplish His will, He simply diversified their language.

In actuality, what happened was that man was allowed to have access to a multiplicity of doctrines. We can certainly give credence to the fact that man, in his relation with God, is as confused as ever. With the diversified doctrines, came many national entities, borders, boundaries, competitions and disputes. With it also came a ruling class called politicians.

These highly skilled manipulators excel in expounding upon a truthful sounding lie. They negotiate peace agreements that can be interpreted differently by all parties. They devise contracts that cannot be understood by the layman; they have to hire a skilled lawyer to tell them what is really meant by the words contained therein. The contract does not say what one thinks it says. Humanity has certainly been cursed through the introduction of diverse tongues and adverse doctrines. The capabilities of a united humanity would be utopian. No problems would be unsolvable. Peace would abound. Happiness would be the norm. Is this a dream, or attainable goal? Will there ever be oneness again - one God, one doctrine... one FAITH? I can truthfully say, it is not only possible, it is on the horizon of the New World Order that is near at hand. How will it happen? Soon you will all become Sons and Daughters of God in a world governed by men governed by God.

In this final portion of the pathway to faith, we shall take a futuristic journey into the days of the Kingdom of God. The Hebrew consonants will again shed the necessary light on our path.

לאוֹם - (Le-O-M) *Place of Birth*

לאוֹמבוּת - (Le-Oo-Mah-Noot) *Nationalism*

לאוֹמבי - (Le-Oo-Mah-Ne) *Nationalistic*

In the days to come it will be a necessity for us to be of one faith under God. We must be released from the bonds of competition to enjoy the freedom of complementing. Nationalism is defined as a sense of national consciousness exalting one nation above all the others, and placing primary emphasis on promotion of its culture and interests, as opposed to those of other "nations."

Understanding the above definition enlightens us as to the subtle changing of the national consciousness of Africans/African Americans to French, British, Americans, etc. through the educational (faith) process. While confessing that education is the heart of a society, we know that it must be the right education. Thereby we find that faith ultimately determines the nationality or national origin of your soul: citizenship, birthplace and geographical boundaries become insignificant. The greater influence is the objective of the institutions of learning. To give you more precise understanding of the three Hebrew words listed above, I will begin with the first word, which is...

21

*לְאֹם - (Le-O-M) *place of birth (nationality)*

It simply refers to the geographical boundary within which one is born, that it may be known to all, his tribal or national birthplace. The distinction between place of birth and ultimate nationality must be made clear. The former refer to geographical location; the latter to the mind of the individual. You should also be aware that even in accordance to the United Nation's Universal Declaration of Human Rights (Article 15), an individual has the right to choose his own nationality, <u>regardless</u> of his birthplace.

To say "I am Yoruba" means to have been born to Yoruba parents or in the Yoruba region. Nigeria may be the initial land of his birth, but his nationalism (true nationality) will only be determined in the years to come.

> *"Train up a child in the way he should go and when he is old, he will not depart from it."*

Proverbs 22:6

We are therefore admonished to take notice of his training. Why?

> *"Beware of false prophets, who come to you in sheep's clothing, but inwardly they are ravening wolves.*
>
> *Ye shall know them by their fruits. Do men gather grapes of thorns, or figs of thistle?*
>
> *Even so, every good tree bringeth forth good fruit but a corrupt tree bringeth forth bad fruit.*
>
> *A good tree cannot bring forth bad fruit, neither can a corrupt tree bring forth good fruit. Every tree that bringeth not forth good*

---

* Here we find that the final consonant (ן) of the root (אֹמֶן) is not present. We also find a prime example of the profundity of the Hebrew thought. For as explained, place of birth (nationality) **לְאֹם***) differs from nationalism* **לְאֹמִבוּה***), and nationalistic* **לְאֹמִבִי***). The latter concept and attribute can only be embraced when subjected to further development (training/education).*

Likewise, only when place of birth (nationality) **לְאֹם***) is subjected to further development in the Hebrew thought, does the final consonant reappear.*

22

fruit is hewn down, and cast into the fire. Wherefore, by their fruits ye shall know them."

Matthew 7:15-20

"While he yet talked to the people, behold, his mother and his brethren stood outside desiring to speak with him.

Then one said unto him. Behold thy mother and thy brethren stand outside, desiring to speak to thee.

But he answered and said unto him that told him, Who is my mother? And who are my brethren?

And he stretched forth his hand toward his disciples, and said, behold my mother and my brethren!

For whosoever shall do the will of my Father, who is in heaven, the same is my brother, and sister, and mother."

Matthew 12:46-50

You may name the tree according to the fruit it bears. An African tree has to bear African fruit. Yeshua is connecting nationality with FAITH (mind) in the above-mentioned verses.

לאומני-(Le-Oo-Mah-Ne) *nationalistic*

לאומיות- (Le-Oo-Mah-Noot) *nationalism*

His training will determine to which nation he belongs. At the root of his national ambitions, we again find faith's root Hebrew consonants (אמן). Upon returning from his training abroad, the African's major objective is to convince his people that he has not returned to swiftly re-adjust and serve. Instead, he returns to be served and to find ways of maintaining his imagined lofty status. The same phenomenon has been observed in the African-American. He no longer feels he belongs to the neighborhood or to its people. In both instances, it is clear that these Africans have subtly (although consistently) been made to feel very insecure with being who they are - Africans! These well-educated, lost souls need keep in mind that individualism runs contrary to nationalism. No matter one's position or status, the individual must always remember that he is an integral part of the greater nation as a whole.

Today, the task of re-creating the African is a challenge for God alone. Social stratification and the "soul transformation" (breaking of the African allegiance) have left us fragmented and small in number... truly a feeble remnant.

Nevertheless, we are the generation faced with the stark realities. We must make some serious resolutions in the 1990s. These critical decisions, affecting the future of Africa and all of God's children, must be tempered with new understanding of nationality and faith.

We now reach the final stage...

אֱמוּנָה- (Eh-Moo-Nah) *trust; firmness; steadfastness; FAITH!*

> *"What doth it profit, my brethren, though a man say he hath faith, and have not works? Can faith save him?*
>
> *If a brother or sister be naked, and destitute of daily food, and one of you say unto them, depart in peace, be ye warmed and filled;*
>
> *Notwithstanding, ye give them not those things which are needful to the body, what doth it profit?*
>
> *Even so faith, if it hath not works, is dead, being alone."*
>
> **James 2:14-17**

Yeshua taught that faith the size of a "mustard seed" could cause an entire mountain to move out of its place. How then has the mountain of problems confronting Africans at home and in the diaspora remained so firmly in place, and apparently unmovable? I pose certain questions through which we may find the answer.

Do you trust in the God of your fathers? Have you been steadfast in maintaining His way? Do you believe in the African mind? Can an African or African institution train you? Are you diligent in your support of African institutions? Do you make others believe in the African mind, while confirming your own confidence in it? Can we guide you and your choice while you attend foreign institutions in pursuit of training not available in your own country? Can we rely upon you to return home after graduation to accept your responsibilities? Are your energies at the disposal of your government and countrymen? Can your country invest more in your education making you a master of your field of expertise? Finally, after the process of learning is completed, where is your allegiance? Has the educational process left you with a deeply ingrained inferiority complex and suppressed your natural, nationalistic tendencies?

At this point, we have arrived at a solution to Africa's current host of problems. Explaining to the apostles the reason for their failure to cast out a similar demon (problem), He (Yeshua) stated: ". . . Because of your unbelief: for verily I say unto you, If ye have faith as a grain of mustard seed, ye shall say unto this mountain, Remove hence to yonder place; and it shall remove; and nothing shall be impossible unto you." Matthew 17:20

Consider the above verses. In your private conversations you state your love for Africa. From your London flat you proclaim her vast wealth. You marvel at her beauty and mysteries. Yet you have not given her that which is needed. Thus what doth it profit? Your words without the aforementioned works are dead, being alone.

"But wilt thou know, O vain man, that faith without works is dead?

Was not Abraham, our father, justified by works, when he had offered Isaac, his son, upon the alter?

Seest thou how faith wrought with his works, and by works was faith made perfect?

And the scripture was fulfilled which saith, Abraham believed God, and it was imputed unto him for righteousness; and he was called the friend of God.

Ye see, then, that by works a man is justified, and not by faith only.

In like manner also was not Rahad, the harlot, justified by works, when she had received the messengers, and she sent them out another way?

For as the body without the spirit is dead, so faith without works is dead also."

James 2:20-26

Are you a friend of Africa, ready to make the sacrifice required of you? You cannot just expect Africa to take her proper place as head of the nations except that you take your place at the head of Africa. We must build a strong Africa, not a stronger Europe in Africa. Without an African spirit (God mind), your body (and all hope for our future) is dead, being alone.

When you say you have faith in an individual or country, then you must be obedient to all the aspects of faith we have discussed. You must allow them to teach you and guide you. Then, by following their instructions, you prove your faith in their guidance, and, in turn, will cause others to believe in them. This is the way you give honor to your country. When you have done these things, your country will know it can rely on you, for you are faithful. You will have found "faith."

"And they that be wise shall shine like the brightness of the firmament; and they that turn many to righteousness, as the stars forever and ever."

Daniel 12:3

"Wash yourselves make yourselves clean; put away the evil of your doings from before mine eyes; cease to do evil;

Learn to do well; seek justice, relieve the oppressed, judge the fatherless, plead for the widow.

Come now, and let us reason together, saith the Lord: though your sins be as scarlet, they shall be as white as snow; though they be red like crimson, they shall be as wool.

If ye be willing and obedient, ye shall eat the good of the land.

But if ye refuse and rebel, ye shall be devoured with the sword: for the mouth of the Lord hath spoken it."

Isaiah 1:16-20

The Attributes
That Lead To . . . Faith

Root Consonants: . . . . (נ) אמן

Confirm, verify, verify
your belief, to educate, to train . . . . לאמן

Training, practice, confirmation . . . . אימון

To believe, to trust by
causing others to believe . . . . להאמין

Faithful, trustworthy, reliable . . . . נאמן

Trainer, educator, ... אומן or אוּ·מן
craftsman, artisan, master

Place of Birth (Nationality) . . . . לאום

Nationalism . . . . לאומנות

Nationalistic . . . . לאומני

Trust, firmness, steadfastness, <u>FAITH</u> . . . . . . אמונה

THE FAMINE

"And these words, which I command thee this day, shall be in thine heart;

And thou shalt teach them diligently unto thy children, and shalt talk of them when thou sittest in thine house, and when thou walkest by the way, and when thou liest down, and when thou risest up.

And thou shalt bind them for a sign upon thine hand, and they shall be as frontlets between thine eyes.

And thou shalt write them upon the posts of thy house, and on thy gates."

Deuteronomy 6:6-9

"And he humbled thee, and suffered thee to hunger, and fed thee with manna, which thou knewest not, neither did thy fathers know; that he might make thee know that man doth not live by bread only, but by every word that proceedeth out of the mouth of the Lord doth man live."

Deuteronomy 8:3

"Behold, the days come, saith the Lord God, that I will send a famine in the land, not a famine of bread, nor a thirst for water, but of hearing the words of the Lord:

And they shall wander from sea to sea, and from the north even to the east they shall run to and fro to seek the word of the Lord, and shall not find it."

Amos 8:11-12

"Pleasant words are as an honey-comb, sweet to the soul, and health to the bones."

Proverbs 16:24

"My son, attend to my words; incline thine ear unto my sayings.

Let them not depart from thine eyes; keep them in the midst of thine heart.

For they are life unto those that find them, and health to all their flesh."

Proverbs 4: 20-22

"A sound heart is the life of the flesh but envy the rottenness of the bones."

Proverbs 14:30

"A merry heart doeth good like a medicine but a broken spirit drieth the bones."

Proverbs 17:22

Perhaps the preceding scriptures are somewhat ambiguous to you. If so, I would attribute your Euro-centric religious teachings as the primary cause, because they have tranquilized your mind and alienated you from God. Subsequently, it is very hard for you to accept that contemporary Christianity isn't in any sense of the word redemp-

29

tive. When an individual is estranged from God, his first inclination is to condone unrighteousness and justify evil. Why has truth become so complicated and hard to comprehend or believe? The truth of the matter is since the first sin of Adam and Eve, righteousness has diminished, and ebbed away. Truth is steadily waning. The proliferation of truth has all but ceased in the earth. Truth can be propagated only by believers of truth and they are very rare.

What is truth? Truth consists of those words, doctrines, outlooks and visions which keep man in harmony with the processes that sustain life eternal. Truth provides the essential body energy for the performing of the will of the Holy One of Israel. Truth comes to man from God and is directly supplied by the Holy Spirit. No man can experience true life and living without it.

Most of us residing on this planet earth have become all too familiar with the term "famine" and the concomitant effects upon those stricken. Severe malnutrition is the most common term used to describe the initial stages of a condition that will have long range, far reaching consequences. My mention of famine is simply to remind you of the devastation it wreaks upon both man and environment.

Your ability to reflect upon the scenario created by a famine of bread will greatly assist you in understanding the aftermath of the famine of hearing the word (truth) of God. The brain (mind) has to be nourished by the ingestion of words of truth. Without this critical intake of the word of God (truth), severe malnutrition is inevitable, leaving man's mind (brain) dysfunctional, not able to carry out even menial tasks in harmony with the will of God. Even very simple truths are now very hard for the stricken human family to understand. Words are actually things; items of food that provide essential vitamins and minerals to your brain. Words are things without motion. When you are continuously exposed to words, they are subsequently energized. This increase of energy will soon require motion. This motion will manifest the tangible. Do you recall the very familiar statements: "Who told you those things?" or "You've been listening to the wrong things!" I now must call your attention to the eternal great commandment which begins with the word "Hear...." The Lord our God is one, and you must love Him with all of your heart, soul and might. Also, within the context of the great commandment (Deuteronomy 6:4-9) we find: And these words which I speak unto you shall be in thine heart and thou shall speak of them when thou liest down, riseth up, when thou sittest in the house or walketh by the way. They shall be for your aspirations (frontlets before your eyes) and vision; you shall also use or refer to them in governing your home and your environment. That is to say, that we/our lives are to be completely encompassed with certain words, ideologies and philosophies.

These spoken words are the initial source of all required vitamins and minerals. In considering this further, let us examine the effects that disposition has on bones and the quality or quantitive effects on the blood produced in the bone marrow. Bone is in a constant process of formation resorption and remodeling. Its growth is regulated by a host of growth regulatory factors which increase the rate of formation, density and other characteristics of bone. We definitely would be remiss if we do not consider the spiritual regulator factor mentioned by Solomon in the preceding scriptural reference. Here we are told that pleasant words are health to the bones, while envy causes the bones to be brittle. We can certainly discern the distinctively different effects that pleasant words (joyful disposition) and envy have on the bones.

Let us consider this scenario. Parathyroid hormone (PTH) is secreted from the parathyroid gland in the neck. It regulates the uptake of calcium from the gut and excretion of calcium in the kidney.

Is it a coincidence that the parathyroid gland is located in an area greatly affected by laughter, joy and happiness and pleasant conversation? Is not the shoulder area greatly affected by tenseness, wherein a shoulder massage can be very relaxing during or after tension (tightness)? Does an evil disposition contribute to the forming of kidney stones caused by an irregular parathyroid hormone secretion? Does the Western culture of tight-buttoned collar and necktie in the area of the parathyroid gland also contribute to bone disease? What is the message being conveyed to us concerning a merry heart and blood production in the bone marrow? Is the mention of "drieth the bones" referring to a possible negative effect upon the quality or quantity of your blood being produced in your bone marrow? Where-

31

fore, since the blood is the life of all of your organs, could the effects of bad spiritual blood be causing problems and ailments in other, even remote places in your internal organs?

Here again we bear witness to the infinite wisdom of the Holy One of Israel in the inspired words of His messengers. We can see the consistency of His truth that psychology, physiology and physiognomy are all controlled by the Word of God and the Law of Relativity. He that has ears to hear, let him hear.

Man's preference now is for the consumption of darkness (i.e., evil, polemical confusion, ignorance, unrighteousness). He readily consumes lies and evil as a result of deception's perversion of his soul, never considering that he is required to yield some measure of his own well-being in exchange for even momentary pleasure. Man now unabatedly consumes perverted substitutes to God's intended rules for living because the lies sound reasonable and truthful. They are made readily available through popular mediums like T.V. and books and require little if any change of character and lifestyle. Surely the reason you turn a blind eye to the wicked, degenerate evil you witness on television is because you recognize the foul-mouth, sex-obsessed characters on your popular T.V. shows as people you know or want to be like. What could be wrong with a little cursing or nudity especially since the church rarely condemns these things. That is the reason the apostate church is still popular. The church is not restrictive. It doesn't require change or denial of things familiar.

Contemporary Euro-centric man has mastered the fabrication of the sacred lie and respectful liars. It is for this reason that the resurrection of the masters (the teachers of God's truth) is so essential. They have come to make the way straight again. The Truth (as God has sanctioned) has been obscured in a nonaccessible corner while the shelves are brimming with decadent deceit. My words, the gospel of the Kingdom of God, are to make you aware of today's real world and what is happening to you when you are subjected to the lie-instigated changes wrought by your pursuit of materialism instead of spiritualism. My objective is to stimulate the fear of what the future holds for you if things continue as they are now going. The Truth, as God intended, alone can provide the congenial, friendly atmosphere required by man's living soul. Without a sufficient amount of truth, body synergism will be put off balance, diminishing sooner or later the development of a strong immune system resulting in the proliferation of disease.

Consider when Yeshua spoke of Nicodemus being born again. He merely was implying that Nicodemus was dead because of the untruths that had influenced his mode of thinking. His eyes saw (perceived) things differently. His feet moved on a path away from God, and his hands worked for another (ungodly) objective. Except that a man has been born again in truth - to perceive, understand and do right - he cannot manifest truth. Truth is the only resurrector of the spiritually dead. The tree of life bears the fruit of righteousness. Therefore, unless one is nourished from this tree, he is considered dead unto God.

Formerly these teachings were given as the guiding light for God's people. Their words and deeds substantiated that they were the people of God unto all that encountered them. They were ensconced by a creative power that forms a protective shield around man when he possesses the knowledge of truth.

I would, at this point, like to further my exegesis on the aforementioned scriptural references and illustrate more fully what living this truth entails. I will begin by acknowledging how proper hygiene and health are linked to truth; that dis-ease reflects body and mind poisoning. This poisoning results when some form of the un-natural or ungodly enter into the blood stream. No sickness or disease develops through osmosis. There has to be a cause. When an organism is affected by poison, some form of damage has to show up in tissue or the organ itself. If the poisons are not eliminated from the body (mind), we will find ourselves fighting an almost hopeless war on misery and disease (which we ourselves or our environment have created and which will ultimately cause premature death).

The prophets Amos and Moses remind us that disease begins with the ingestion of falsehood, the father of negative thoughts. This falsehood affects the digestion and metabolism of all foods consumed. The psychological factor also influences the onset of depression, stress and fatigue. The teachings of Amos and Moses preclude the onset of disease by the secondary consumption of the herbs of the field. In every instance (other than purposeful poisoning and contamination of water, etc.), the provenance of disease in the organism is caused by a lethal frame of mind. If we can accept this very essential truth, we may also discover that the principal contributor to our physical demise is whomever it is that has been implanting lies in our minds. Erroneous words, anti-God doctrine and vain conversing has caused much more disease than poor eating habits.

Have you ever stopped to give a thorough analysis to the oft-used and heard phrase "You make me sick!"? Can the things others do or say really cause you to get sick? Could there be other things classified as or similar to "passive smoking?" Is there such a thing as a "passive lecture" or a "passive speech?" What affect does the continuous hearing of predominantly erroneous doctrines have on the digestion and metabolism of your food and other components of the life element?

As a way of illustrating this point, let us consider the effect trees have on the quality of air man breathes and the rain he receives when trees emit oxygen into the atmosphere. Moreover, this same air and rain is essential for the life of the tree also. Conversely, take a hypothetical look at a tree that contaminates its own environment. Ultimately its oxygen and rain output will be negatively affected and could possibly cause its own premature destruction. Consequently the tree has to always "remember" that it is an essential part of the larger forest and that by poisoning its own eco-system, it could negatively effect other trees that share its habitat.

Let us now consider man, symbolized in the Bible as a tree. As an integral part of the Creation, the tree (man) is placed in a cycle which requires him to provide essential ingredients to sustain his life. What should man therefore feel in regard to his environment, considering that he is so inextricably linked to nature? Is there a fundamental doctrine or series of words whose use is imperative to ensuring man's existence? Do these words interact with other unseen components of the universe that protect his growth and development, e.g., as does the oxygen which forms the rain that in turn waters his land, from which he receives his nourishment?

How did man allow deadly individualism to creep in, causing him to forget that he is part and parcel of the greater forest? He now makes others sick where once, when in harmony with his God, he made others well. You are absolutely correct in your use of the statement "You make me sick!" You merely lack an understanding of the extent of the damage being done. The words of your neighbors or children arguing are making you sick; the altercation down the street and the drive-by shootings in the inner city are making you sick.

All of the negative things being said and done around you generate deadly toxins that enter the bloodstream. Thus begins a degenerative process that impedes the function of your organs and affects the body's proper chemical reactions within the cycles of life. Toxic physical bodies must be detoxified to give ailing organs a chance to regenerate. When the body has been overrun by toxins, the mind has to be purged. The only hope is to be born again.

Deception is the most common man-made virus being injected into the human organism through the process of institutionalized mis-education. Can disease be transmitted in a classroom? Certainly! Consider, genes are segments of DNA that contain (must receive) instructions to make proteins, the building blocks of life. Things heard can cause extreme headaches. Certain spoken words can immediately increase blood pressure and the flow of adrenalin. We've certainly heard of heart attacks coming as a result of unexpected well-kept secrets being suddenly exposed. This is sufficient evidence that words alone can cause extreme negative physical reactions.

What I'm implying is that just as one acquires historical knowledge and reading and writing skills in a classroom, subjecting one's self to the bombardment of lies can cause lung disease, kidney failure, strokes, heart attacks, etc. The course is sometimes referred to by the misleading title "life management" instead of "death causing."

Lies, little children, are not something deciduous, you hear and walk away from. Falsehood drains essential energy from the body, thereby weakening the body's resistance to disease. Let us delve further in our perusal of the effect of words on health to include sound. Does music dictate the way one dances? Absolutely! Just as music puts often irresistible demands on your body, likewise words, doctrines, ideologies, philosophies and various viewpoints exact involuntary demands of your physiology. Reggae music solicits special feet and body movements; likewise do highlife, jazz, rap and the present heavy metal sound. The words/sounds take complete control of body movement and feelings.

The most significant cause of ill health in man is his over-exposure to lies and liars. This causes habitual errors of one kind or another, the immediate results of which are not felt nor generally intelligently evaluated. You may suffer verbal abuse for years and feel no pain. The cumulative damage, however subtle, is sufficient to impede your understanding of my urgent call for a spiritual dietary change. Let me give you an illustration of how lies can effect your health. Take for instance the lie about what constitutes good eating. Many people, have been convinced that a juicy red steak, or a side of pork spare ribs smothered in barbecue sauce is good eating. This is a lie. Simply being in the presence of someone continuously saying or implying that you can or should eat swine flesh can/will cause sickness and disease whether you consume it or not. This is the critical area or source of ill feelings that is almost always overlooked. Truth, subsequently, becomes like an excellent diet, it prevents the onset of disease and can be medicinal in he who speaks it and he who believes it. We are now better able to gauge the extent of damage that was/is being caused by the famine of hearing the word (truth) of God.

The eating of meat is the best illustration I can give of a habitual error whose immediate results won't always be felt. But if you continue to eat chemically-injected decaying, indigestible, colon-clogging, cancer-inducing meats, believe me, you can order your grave plot now because you'll be needing it sooner than you realize. Sure, meat may taste good and may satisfy your appetite, but God did not create man's digestive tracts to accommodate meat. Carnivorous animals have short intestines which enable meats to be quickly expelled. Humans, however, have exceptionally long intestinal tracts which cannot withstand the decaying of meats which linger inside us. Nevertheless, the time will definitely come when the organs will rebel, making you consciously aware of a diseased condition manifest in a major organ or in some other remote place weakened by malnutrition (the ingestion of irritating toxic words accumulated beyond the mind's overworked eliminative powers). It is the constant bombardment of erroneous teachings and falsehoods, that activates negative reactions which, in most cases, are responsible for the gradual erosion and ultimate destruction of health. Lying is, and causes, chronic disease. When lying is chronic, its negative force is constantly vexing and weakening. The next logical question will more than likely be: what and whom is the chronic liar weakening? I can comfortably and accurately respond that he is/has made himself sick and all others that regularly listen to him. Just consider: your life cycles and all of your inner organs revolving around a lie! Consequently, whoever teaches you falsehoods - the Christmas lie, the Easter lie, the Sunday-as-the-Sabbath day lie, the flesh-consumption-is-safe lie, etc. - is literally proliferating disease. If you are a liar or constantly in the company of a liar or liars, you're going to pay the price in a debilitating disease.

I believe this gospel of the Kingdom. The fear (truth) of the Lord prolongeth days, but the years of the wicked shall be shortened. Words of truth provide health to your soul. The prophets have testified that pleasant words can influence the health of those who hear them. We have likewise been warned to spend little to no time in the presence of those who are continuously blurting out evil (lies and deceit). Remember, the mouth plants the seeds (words) that determine the nutritional yield of the foods that are consumed.

"A man shall eat good by the fruit of his mouth, but the soul of the transgressors shall eat violence."

"Go from the presence of a foolish man, when thou perceivest not in him the lips of knowledge."

Proverbs 13:2;14:7

If you consume toxic doctrines, as many do in the apostate church, you will (if you have not already) eventually become sick and completely miss the true pleasure of life with a living, vibrant soul. First the quality of life will be reduced until it becomes worthless, leading you to your certain premature death. Nevertheless, not all is lost; there is hope that you may hear this gospel of the Kingdom of God.

Not everyone that is lost need remain so. If you are to transform your life of uncertainty you will have to challenge your own traditional beliefs, initially by just being bold enough to search the scriptures and historical records in pursuit of truth. Once you've discovered the truth, then you are at your hour of decision. Should you/can you make the necessary change after believing a lie for so many years? Here I must again remind you that the greatest obstacle to a man being born again is the embarrassment he must face concerning his own past. To encourage you however, I might add that with even your first step in the opposite direction, you begin to reverse the sentence of unhappiness, sickness and certain premature degeneration. Toxic physical bodies must be detoxified. Such is also the case with a toxic mind. Disease in the body is an indication of the presence of internal mental filth; it is a natural body process, the organism's reaction to the toxic state it is now experiencing at an unacceptable level. Truth and discipline are the essential prescriptions for spiritual and physical regeneration. They cannot be circumvented in the absolute healing process.

> *"Stay yourselves, and wonder; cry out, and cry; they are drunk, but not with wine; they stagger, but not with strong drink."*
>
> **Isaiah 29:9**

> *"Now go, write it before them on a tablet, and note it in a book, that it may be for the time to come forever and ever,*
>
> *That this is a rebellious people, lying children, children who will not hear the law of the Lord;*
>
> *Who say to the seers, See not; and to the prophets, Prophesy not unto us right things; speak unto us smooth things, prophesy deceits;"*
>
> **Isaiah 30:8-10**

We take note here that the inspired prophet of God has made special mention of the people of God being drunk, but not from strong drink. What do you assume is the cause of this stupifying intoxication? Whatever it is, we may agree on two salient points: first, they've had too much of it, and second, it has brought upon them a condition that does not find pleasure in the eyes of God. I conclude that they are drunk from false indoctrination. Deception has blurred their eyes, made them weak and caused them to do foolish things (as would a drunkard).

The evil social system attempts to encourage such behavior by alluding to getting/being "high" as fun. These words of the prophet Isaiah are a perfect description of the African born in America at this point in history. He "stumbles as a blind man at noonday." He is in fact not high, but low from the over-indulgence of Draconian, foreign and evil doctrines. He has abrogated the authority and control of his soul to the devil. Gradually, he has become more and more accustomed to lies, smooth but lethal words. His health and national welfare have deteriorated in exact proportion to the quantity of lies consumed. He is a perfect illustration of how, from a carnal perspective, when junk food is consumed, inferior thoughts are produced. Fast foods (deceit) in, deception out. In his present state of intoxication, God-consciousness is more an illusion than a reality.

The mentally sick are largely the product of culinary "art": the art of making hot dogs, potato and corn chips, "Big Macs," cotton (sugar) candy, doughnuts, carbonated and chemicalized drinks, and sugar-laden cereals that "snap, crackle and pop" but offer little in the way of nourishing bodies and minds.

The high-minded European (and Euro-centrically-influenced) peoples of the world sport their fancy titles, pompous positions and pious religions while their civilizations fall apart under the influence of err and the deceived human family writhes in agony from an array of virulent diseases that afflict them. In retrospect, as we now consider the words of the inspired prophets of God, the effect of the *famine* of the Word of God on the human family has become clear. The scarcity of truth and the proliferation of lies has been devastating. The most extensive damage caused by this famine is found in the malnourished minds of the children. In many cases, sadly, the damage is irreversible. Prophetically speaking, the physical and spiritual condition of the adults has brought forth this evil degenerate generation.

Remember, after a prolonged *famine*, an individual will consume almost anything. He is no longer able to rationalize with his mind; he can only answer the desire of his flesh. So it is with contemporary Euro-centric men and their diabolical mentality. They only understand and seek to fulfill the lust of the flesh. This is the direct result of a dysfunctional mind caused by a severe *famine* of truth.

The fallen African Edenic family has been possessed by a Euro-centric, anti-God mind that is infected with an aversion to truth. The words they desire to hear are likened unto the things they prefer to eat: foods that are inferior in quality. Their approach to life is disjointed and irrational as if their physical and mental (spiritual) consumption (diet) has nothing to do with their health. It is evident that right words spoken properly provide nourishment to one's soul. Consequently, improper consumption of wrong words causes malnutrition and spiritual malfunction. The relationship between hearing and speaking lies and evil, and disease and immorality is clear and irrefutable. The masses are suffering from spiritual malnutrition - a lack of the Divine knowledge required to nourish the in-dwelling spirit of God.

We are being bombarded daily by so-called health experts that explain the nutritional requirements of the body, yet there is very little governmental support for healthful eating. With relative scrutiny, we will discern the same spirit of err involved in matters of spiritual nourishment. As in the liberal democratic social system, it does not matter to them what you eat; everything is made available, the right and wrong. We must remember that almost too much of anything can be unhealthy. It is very doubtful that people can even keep track of all of the dietary guidelines, news reports and food advertisements telling them what they should or should not be eating. They are often confusing and contradictory, owing to unethical politics and business, further alienating the people from the truth. Though drowning in information, they are starving for true knowledge!

It is the same strategy being used with spirituality, in that there are more than 2,000 religions in America alone, and more than 10,000 world-wide. It does not matter what God you worship or how you worship him. This obviously encourages confusion and deception but that was/is the devil's objective.

If a lack of hearing of the word of God causes a famine, then a preponderance of truth (the word of God) can be likened unto a continuous supply of food. Thus, it does not require much imagination to conclude that the source of such nourishment has to be spiritual men anointed by God. Take heed, for if man does not live by bread alone, it stands to reason that he does not get sick, suffer and die by the lack of bread alone. He that has ears to hear, let him hear.

In the course of my dissertation, I must continue to emphasize that there are universal laws that govern man's existence on this planet. These laws cannot be circumvented without penalty. When a law is violated, there will always be a relative response. The character of man molds his environment, determines his friends and enemies, and greatly affects the state of his health. Every man, woman and child bear the outward mark of their adherence to or disregard of these laws as revealed by their figures, their postures, their countenances, and their attitudes toward life and fellowman.

The knowledgeable eyes of spiritual men governed by God, closely monitoring the physiognomy of those who have turned aside, can discern their lifestyles as clearly as they can the lines and symbols of a road map. The logical question would seem to be: how could any other rationale prevail? I rationalize that only through a return unto God and obedience to His laws will man succeed in removing the ominous, destructive clouds that hover overhead. When we honestly and soberly seek a harmonious relationship with nature and fellowman, we are required to recognize the existence of faults in our lifestyle and correct them expediently.

Sin, although universally practiced and accepted, still pays the wages of death. Even scientific data serves to demonstrate that when man deviates from God's (nature's) prescribed plan, the life process is impaired. Relative problems then follow, which are the natural result of his deviation. Man in his very obvious evil society is in need of an infusion of truth. There is no shortcut or easy way: man has been greatly deceived. It's a bitter pill, but he eventually must purge his body and mind with the bitter cleanser of truth and accept the embarrassment. The dysfunction of contemporary man's mind and the motivation which negatively affects his soul has been caused by

41

his alienation from God. Thinking that he was becoming wise, he trapped himself and all of his constituents in gross darkness. All of those that desire to live must open their ears, hearts and minds for the ingestion and digestion of truth as put forth by men anointed by God.

"And ye shall know the truth, and the truth shall make you free."

John 8:32

If truth will set you free, then truth becomes a/the principal weapon in a freedom struggle. But, again, what is truth? I reason that if the use of truth is required to set us free, then someone has to know truth. Furthermore, when heard, it has to be comprehensible. <u>Truth</u> thus becomes the key to mental, physical, conscious and sub-conscious <u>power</u>.

In the beginning, the living foundation (soul) of all spoken words was truth. Yeshua once said: "let your words be yea or nay." He simply meant for us to be careful regarding verbosity, because if it is not the truth, it will, in the by and by, produce evil results. The substance derived from truth is <u>always</u> beneficial: it unceasingly strengthens, blesses, and exalts everyone who acknowledges and believes in it. It positively affects every object or thing created on earth or within the universal order, i.e, all things created by God were "good" because they stemmed from truth. Everything in existence that yet remains in its primal state has a positive influence on like existing objects. This positive influence has far-reaching consequences, impacting positively on every living person, creature or thing whose foundation is truth.

No matter how articulate, sensible, eloquent, etc. words may sound, if they are not the truth, they will be injurious and/or destructive. As the saying goes, "there are no vain words."

In simple terms, negativity's principal bedfellow is negativity. Light and darkness have no overt association. When light appears, darkness disappears or flees away. Have you ever noticed that where rays of light enter, the shade vanishes. Likewise, the habitat of the righteous (light) is hell for the wicked (darkness). A wicked person that journeys to a foreign land has no problem finding his counterparts in the midst of a multitude. Their evil natures involuntarily attract one to the other.

Similarly it pains the righteous to be in the company of the wicked. A perfect illustration of this fact is shown when Noah built an ark in order to escape the habitation of the wicked of his day. Another illustration can be seen in the examples of Moses when he forsook Egypt, and Abraham, when he desired and sought a place whose maker and builder was God.

Everyone that finds comfort and enjoyment in the fellowship of the wicked inevitably will have a calamitous end. There are many, unfortunately, who have succumbed to the seductive, intoxicating life of evil, ungodly, behavior - adultery, crime, perversion (i.e., homosexuality), lies, and indifference. But be aware, where God's evaluation of your behavior is concerned, there is no compromising or fence straddling. You are either for or against God and that entails adhering to His guidelines in all that you say and do, from the foods you eat (is what you eat slowly destroying your body, or do you demonstrate your love and appreciation for life by eating health-sustaining foods?) to your everyday conversation - do you curse, lie, blaspheme or make negative proclamations continuously? This is just another perspective on the relationship between truth and lie - or between good and evil. You must understand that evil cannot possibly terminate the impregnable will of the righteous. No jail can contain them, no calamity can destroy them. There is absolutely no negative or evil force that can overcome them.

Likewise, with all things of a positive nature and extraction rooted in truth, truth can have no master other than its creator, the Omnipotent God of Israel. There is no force that can imprison or incarcerate it. No power can subdue, suppress, impede or destroy it. Truth is infinite as well as everyone or everything born of its soul. Allow me to illustrate my thesis by using one of God's creation - a watermelon. It is a fruit composed of nature's unadulterated minerals which, when left untampered with by man, has an eternal cycle of existence. It will perpetually remain a nutritious element used to augment continuously, God's creation. The watermelon's continuity is derived from its essence, which is truth.

Let us delve even deeper into the everlasting life or existence of a watermelon. Let us imagine that a watermelon has a mind and thinks and feels like contemporary man. It would probably dread being eaten for fear of annihilation, extinction, or for lack of a better word, death. Comparable to the ways of man, it would spend its days in constant fear of being snuffed out of existence. Every day would be a nightmare, time spent in a state of apprehension; anxiety would consume it continuously. Animosity, jealousy and treachery would undoubtedly arise between watermelons out of their desperation to live a "single" lifetime on earth. Each would strive to live as long and as best as one could in the one cycle or span of time allocated by its creator, the Eternal God.

Sounds far-fetched or ridiculous to you? Certainly it does! However, when we consider how the majority of the world's populace thinks, it doesn't sound so outlandish. This concept of life engulfs the minds of men, women and children worldwide. However, to conceive that the Eternal God is the author of such misery is absurdity and even blasphemy. To think that He would create a man to live a short lifetime, during the course of which he is to worry each day about dying (consciously or unconsciously), is a gross misconception. The founder of such an obviously evil lie or concept has to be the devil.

The devil has deceived the whole world. Whether you care to accept it or not, the world's masses are all imprisoned by a lie. The simple equation is that if truth frees, then a lie confines. Death as defined by the devil is the expiration of the body, but death as defined by God is the expiration of the mind.

One of the greatest challenges of the gospel of the Kingdom is/has been convincing "living" people that they are in fact already dead. For no matter how many times we quote Yeshua's words "the flesh profiteth nothing," relate to Nicodemus being told that he would have "to be born again," or James the chief apostle stating, "the body without the spirit is dead," the greatly deceived masses still lean to the satanic definition of a functioning body equalling life. Likewise, very few if any African Americans will accept without contention that they are in fact <u>prisoners</u> in the ghastly domain of evil, except they are actually incarcerated in a penal institution. American policy-makers have labored unceasingly, indelibly stamping the illusion of freedom on the hearts and minds of her citizens and others to the ends of the earth. Yet truth, in fact, paints another kind of picture of America's liberal democratic social system, one that is despairingly ugly. Deception continues to raise her ugly head, continually causing the human family to believe and accept the ignoble lie, rather than perceive and understand that which is true.

However, the truth is, that death is absolute once wickedness, evil, unrighteousness or an ungodly state of mind dominates the body. The advent of this type of death first occurred to the Sons of God when the God-spirit was alienated from them. Existence at that state is like a ship being tossed against the rocks on a turbulent sea. Every day, ominous clouds hang over the head as a breach ready to break. Life, as such, if it can be defined as life, is an uninterrupted chain of negative threatening feelings that stalk, pursue, and engulf the spiritually dead. There is no escape for the wicked; they can neither commit "hari-kari" (suicide) nor any other form of self-destruction in an attempt to circumvent their hellish state.

All enslavers, exploiters, corrupters, murderers and adulterers cannot escape their fate. Inevitably they shall be continuously resurrected to experience the torment that is the fate of the wicked. This is not a hopeful, imaginary belief, but an inevitable reality.

The resurrection is not in some distant remote time, but occurs almost instantly. When an evil man dies - the unrighteous spirit leaves a body that succumbs prematurely, or that is too feeble to contain it - where does the spirit go? If an unrighteous spirit abandons a ramshackled vessel it finds refuge to continue its existence in another compatible vessel, one just born or already in existence. That is to say, it is foolish to think that a man (spirit) like Hitler can create the havoc which he wreaked upon earth in his short lifetime and simply die, never to reap the harvest of his work. He, nor any other unrighteous spirit, has escaped the judgment of God. At this stage of the development of the Kingdom of God, they justly inherit an unrighteous state of existence; reaping continuously all of the

45

ramifications of the evil they have sown. The hell which such a spirit creates shall in turn be its perpetual habitation. If you live by the sword, by the sword you shall die. If you are the author of misery, then misery shall be your constant everlasting companion. If you are an exploiter, thief, liar, etc., then these attributes shall pursue you and eventually overtake you in this present life or in the lives of your seed which shall inevitably follows. The world which created the wicked shall be eternally tormented by the wicked.

We have ofttimes heard the secular expression "history repeats itself." However, how would an anointed spiritual man interpret such a statement? Is history repeating itself, or is it an evil spirit continuously repeating itself?

> *"For the ways of man are before the eyes of the Lord, and he pondereth all his goings.*
>
> *His own iniquities shall take the wicked himself, and he shall be held with the cords of his sins. "*
>
> **Proverbs 5:21-22**

I can certainly bear witness on behalf of my people that the spirit of the evil ruler Antiochus* has been prevalent and present until this very day, trying to alter the laws of God and prevent us from keeping them. He decreed that the people of God should be put to death if they would keep or even learn and advocate the keeping of the laws of God. He compelled them to profane the holy sabbath day, adopt and keep the laws of his/a strange new religion. He used the swine (pig) to defile the altar of God and continued his campaign to make the pig acceptable for consumption by the people of God. Thus, we may correctly conclude that it is the spirit that is continuously repeating itself.

Again let us return to the watermelon, a product created by the Holy One of Israel in order to fortify the health of man. It was given an endless cycle of existence. This state would exist eternally, as long as the watermelon remains in the perfect or truthful cycle of nature.

*Antiochus IV, King of Syria 175-167 B.C.E.

46

Certainly if a watermelon is created by the Holy One of Israel in such a way that its life-cycle is eternal, then how much more the life-cycle of man, who was created in His image and likeness? The author of deception and delusion has been the major cause of man's troublesome plight. His lies are perceived as the truth. The spirit of err is the source or soul of all evil, also referred to as the devil. The devil is a spirit, and is activated by lies. God is a spirit that is motivated by the truth, the spoken and written word of God.

> *"But the hour cometh, and now is, when the true worshipers shall worship the Father in spirit and in truth; for the Father seeketh such to worship him.*
>
> *God is a Spirit; and they that worship him must worship him in spirit and in truth."*

John 4:23-24

> *"In the beginning was the Word, and the Word was with God and the Word was God."*

John 1:1

In the beginning was the word (Truth)...

Lies - the seed of the wicked - are presently on the threshold of absolute destruction. Truth has now become the rule or standard which man must live by. When the rich man beseeched Abraham to allow him to go and tell his relatives how to circumvent going to hell, Abraham replied unto him: "They have Moses and the prophets. Let your relatives hear them (obey them)."

Regretfully, the very gullible human family is prone to protect "what I've believed all my life," and defend the privileged place of lies, no matter how detrimental these prevarications are to life. So passion runs high and the real issues are obscured. Nevertheless, what do you do with truth after you hear it? Your first realization has to be that in a world rotating upon the axis of a lie, truth has to require or, better yet, demand change. Actually, the acceptance of truth is the beginning of a new creative process. To all who become compliant, it will fashion you into a new person made in the image and likeness of God. Truth is the source of all life. It is found in every living human cell. It is similar to the DNA (deoxyribonucleic acid) molecule found in the nucleus of cells. Only if it is present can the instructions of life be passed into the biological computer. Falsehood is likened unto a two-edged sword. When you speak, you're not only relating information to others; likewise you've sent a message within your own soul. You are killing and dying at the same time.

Truth brings with it the bitter reality that material wealth is vain when spiritual poverty is prevalent. True life cannot/shall not be found in economic growth and prosperity. With your return to sanity and common sense, an inevitable confessional attitude and outlook will prevail. There are obviously faulty social practices and lie-oriented thought patterns that have led to an existence referred to by the prophets as "gross darkness." The limitations of affluent society's money and purchasing power are self-evident in the distressing scenes of armies of wandering homeless in Washington, D.C., the capital of the "wealthiest" nation in human history. Drugs, crime, violence, children having children, gang warfare, racial violence and a plague of sickness are all the fruit of men under the satanic influence of err trying to govern without God.

Certainly America has sent many purchasing agents into the marketplace to buy the solutions to her myriad problems. The federal government spent $2.5 trillion dollars on poverty programs in the last 25 years, trying to buy material solutions to what are spiritual problems. Not only do the problems prevail, but they have significantly expanded their terrain and show the promise of unchecked growth. America's politicians, economists, sociologists, scientists and technicians have all failed. Her only hope is to be found in taking a page from Hebraic history in Egypt and Babylon. She has to seek out the Hebrew advisors anointed by God as did Pharoah and Nebuchadnezzar. In fact, the only hope for the entire human family is to pray, seek to find and do that which is conducive to a closer relationship with God, the keys to which are to be found only in the hands of the Messianic people at Jerusalem.

48

"A new heart also will I give you, and a new spirit will I put within you; and I will take away the stony heart out of your flesh, and I will give you an heart of flesh."

Ezekiel 36:26

"And whatsoever man there is of the children of Israel, or of the strangers who sojourn among you, who hunteth and catcheth any beast or fowl that may be eaten, he shall even pour out the blood thereof, and cover it with dust.

For it is the life of all flesh; the blood of it is for the life thereof: therefore I said unto the children of Israel,

Ye shall eat the blood of no manner of flesh; for the life of all flesh is the blood thereof: whosoever eateth it shall be cut off."

Leviticus 17:13-14

"And he said, Go, and tell this people, hear ye indeed, but understand not; and see ye indeed, but perceive not.

Make the heart of this people fat, and make their ears heavy, and shut their eyes; lest they see with their eyes, and hear with their ears, and understand with their heart, and be converted, and be healed."

Isaiah 6:9-10

"Why should ye be stricken any more? Ye will revolt more and more; the whole head is sick, and the whole heart faint.

From the sole of the foot even unto the head there is no soundness in it, but wounds, and bruises, and putrefying sores. They have not been closed, neither bound up, neither mollified with ointment."

Isaiah 1:5-6

"Is it not yet a very little while, and Lebanon shall be turned into a fruitful field, and the fruitful field shall be esteemed as a forest?

And in that day shall the deaf hear the words of the book, and the eyes of the blind shall see out of obscurity, and out of darkness."

Isaiah 29:17-18

"Therefore my people are gone into captivity, because they have no knowledge; and their honorable men are famished, and their multitude dried up with thirst."

Isaiah 5:13

From the aforementioned scriptural references, we may clearly ascertain the very sordid state of the physical existence of the former Sons of Light. The entire human family, being governed by deception, is subsequently "dead." The prescription? "A blood transfusion to restore health to the inner organism;" "a heart transplant to restore feeling;" "brain surgery for the comprehension of truth." Delicate eye and ear surgery is required for malfunctioning eyes and ears. The surgeons, "those anointed of God."

Everyone that is a part of this present Euro-gentile world system suffers from the above-mentioned maladies. In this virtual hell on earth, those with the conviction that they are living, are suffering from a debilitating mental disorder. This conviction is merely an illusion. Those who programmed them have chained and bound them in a prison on death row. As long as this illusion, this lie, maintains control, it will overwhelmingly convince the mind, influencing the physiological mechanisms to crave the abnormal, causing you to do the abnormal in your entire lifestyle, resulting in abnormal physical disorders and degeneration. The manipulation of your mind will eventually change everything for the better or for worse: what you eat, what you drink, what you wear, how you live, how you die and how you see yourselves in relation to your fate.

"And it shall come to pass, that thou shalt hearken diligently unto the voice of the Lord thy God, to observe and to do all his commandments which I command thee this day, that the Lord thy God will set thee on high above all nations of the earth;

And all these blessings shall come on thee, and overtake thee, if thou shalt hearken unto the voice of the Lord thy God."

"But it shall come to pass if thou wilt not hearken unto the voice of the Lord thy God, to observe to do all his commandments and his statutes which I command thee this day, that all these curses

shall come upon thee, and overtake thee."

Deuteronomy 28:1-2,15

Destiny is defined as "a predetermined course of events often held to be a resistless power or station.." Whoever controls the development of a man's character controls his destiny; that is to say, controls his health and welfare. It is for that reason most of the ailments afflicting the human family are predictable long before they occur, even your old age. But what is a healthy lifestyle? The first question should be, "what is life?" Life begins with the active presence of God guiding you in all that you undertake. "Acknowledge the Lord in all thy ways..." This cannot be found in religiousity, for life and living is not a religion.

The great majority of the earth's inhabitants have allowed their destiny to be controled by those of adverse intentions. The Euro-gentile -- through instilling a decadent, ungodly nature and character -- has guided them into direct conflict with life and living (God). First and foremost, no layman controls his own destiny. His destiny is being controled by those in whom he has placed the confidence to form his character. The character of men is supposed to be formed by spiritual masters that have been endowed with the understanding of the path that leads unto God and the destiny He has chosen for His people. These men control blessings and prevent curses. They are like unto doors: they cannot be circumvented if you desire to enter the domain of holiness. Therefore, if you arrogantly deny or ignore these truths I have scribed, a lie will remain the driving force behind your destiny.

Consider the well known fact that mother's milk strengthens the immune system and promotes a more passive behavior in children. Yet it is the social system that overwhelms the need and/or desire to breastfeed a child. It will not be promoted as ailment and negative behavior planning; yet truthfully that is exactly what is it is. Again, the enemy is well disguised and hard to detect. For example: he insinuates to the mother that breastfeeding is old-fashioned, time consuming and will interfere with her life and freedoms. She then accepts the artificial formula as modern, progressive and just as good or better than mother's milk. The mechanics of evil reasoning (oppo-

51

sition to truth) will have far-reaching effects on the child's life and mind as the mother implants her hidden conviction of what he must experience, preparing his body to conform to it. Destiny requires the seeds that are planted to bear after their kind from infancy to the grave. The artificial world will dominate his/her life. The natural way and/or things of God that should be easy to comprehend will more often than not fall on deaf ears.

We must all come to realize that in every instance, disease in the body comes from something faulty in the mind and spirit. More often than not, it is possible to uncover the principle contributors to man's physical demise. Nevertheless, deceived man has a preference for darkness instead of light, sickness instead of health, and chooses to erroneously believe in a heavenly death instead of a heavenly life. Furthermore, the unmerciful adversary of God, not leaving any stone unturned, proceeded on to fashion a god in the image of the people. This god gives approval or turns a blind eye to their evil lifestyles. He doesn't care what they eat, drink, say, wear, or how they look. Gluttony or other dietary deviancy and its resultant obesity and other problems is of no concern to this god. Nor is he overly concerned about their preference of religious affiliation. They are only required to demonstrate their belief in this false god, and they certainly do... with all of their heart, soul and might.

But who shall believe the report? You are reaping what has been sown. Who has planted the seeds of evil which have yielded this harvest of destruction? If a man does not know when he's living, he doesn't know when he's dying. If you are not clear when you're winning, you're not sure when you're losing. If you cannot identify the source of the evil seeds, destruction will be your eternal harvest.

In the beginning, God created man in His image and likeness. He invested His mind and environment in him. He expected perpetual dividends - eternal Divine stewardship and to remain perpetually in the image of God. When man turned aside, the Almighty God did as any wise investor would do in the face of default: he started dispossessing! What we bear witness to at this time is the aftermath of God's heavy divestment. If God has expropriated his shares and annulled his partnership in the deceived human family, then who is it that has invested so heavily in contemporary man's social systems? The answer is logical: whomever's interest they are promoting. The primary reason that the African born in America hasn't obtained his freedom is that he has not convinced God in word and deed that it is <u>in His best interest</u>.

At this point, let us consider the original God-ordained Messianic Ministry. The Messianic Minister was/is first and foremost the servant of God. The servant is called such because he performs a service for God. We recall hearing the layman apprise us that he was going to attend the "ministerial (church) service." The service was the gathering place for those complying or seeking to learn how to comply with the commands or demands of God. Thus, the servant provided services that benefitted or helped to promote the interest of God in both man and society. The Messianic Minister had truth put at his disposal for use, along with Divine reasoning, as it is written "come now and let us reason together." He was trained to convince those that would hear to invest in projects, areas or things that would increase God's interest. The Anointed Minister was trained and given a list of all things wherein the Almighty God held a vested interest. The people attending the service would make joyful noises in the house of God, always with the objective of trying to convince God to invest in them or with them. Sometimes the spirit was extremely high when someone bore witness of a successful joint venture, testifying that surely God had blessed them beyond imagination. The faithful Messianic Minister would sometimes become very emotional while trying to convince the people to invest in areas wherein God held the controlling interest. On the other hand, he would also issue a stern admonishment: do not partake of or utilize anything not in the interest of God.

Following God's instructions (law) is not a matter of convenience, but is of the utmost necessity in the safe-guarding of our lives. He is the God of the Living. He, therefore, teaches and admonishes us to protect and keep our lives. Therefore, when you are free in God, it does not come without responsibility. The freedom of God entails a moral responsibility. You must develop a sensitivity to what you eat, drink, smell, wear or say, even to what you allow to be eaten, worn, or said in your presence. Remember: the present Euro-centric mentality and culture is promoting the interests of satan! They threaten the basic or fundamental values of life because they oppose the life-giving source and substance: God and truth.

Men were never to be free to commit evil randomly as a norm of their lives. The objective of God is to harness, not free evil. The present world under the guise of "freedom" has freed evil. How does getting in bed on stage and having sex to the sound of thunderous applause become part of an extremely popular entertainment act? How does defecating on stage become popular? Simply because the performers of these acts are free. Free to do evil. Who has freed such spirits? Why were they freed? Are such acts irrelevant or are they relevant to a mind and purpose? Freedom cannot be undefined nor divorced from morality.

The entertainers are trying to satisfy an obvious thirst and hunger for evil. Yet, the thirst seems unquenchable; the appetite unsatiable. How much further can "way out" go? Who would pay an entertainer to come on stage naked, or to defecate and have intercourse on stage? Who could reward them for that but satan? Who could pay royalties to those who write lyrics such as, "Tina got a big ole butt. I know I told you I'd be true. But Tina got a big ole butt, so I'm leaving you."[1] "I'll settle for the back of your hand somewhere on my behind. I don't want you to thank me; you can just spank me."[2] Who would attend concerts where the performers sing such lyrics? Can you imagine an audience of Sons of God clapping and stomping their feet to such an infamy? Who do the above-mentioned work for? Whose payroll are they on?

At some point, we have all come to consider the fundamentals of good business management. That being the case, then we can surely understand that God would not promote the goods of his chief rival or competitor; that's not good business! When it comes to God's business, very little savvy or erudition is displayed. Let us cease from being "scatter-brained" and face the unequivocal reality of this present

[1] *"Big Ole Butt" by L.L. Cool J*
[2] *"Hanky Panky" by Madonna*

world system. Where is the social system today that is promoting the interest of God? Identify the food industry; point out the clothing industry. Would you classify a clothing industry which manufactures unisex garments as promoting the interest of God? If they are not promoting the interest of God, then who are they representing? Doesn't it make good business sense to conclude that they are being helped by, salaried by, and supported by whomever it is they are representing? After all, "no man can serve two masters."

> *"Ye adulterers and adulteresses, know ye not that the friendship of the world is enmity with God? Whosoever, therefore, will be a friend of the world is the enemy of God."*
>
> *" Submit yourselves, therefore, to God. Resist the devil, and he will flee from you.*
>
> *Draw near to God, and he will draw near to you. Cleanse your hands, ye sinners; and purify your hearts, ye double-minded."*
>
> **James 4:4,7-8**

When the Messianic Minister was/is ordained, it was/is merely a ceremonial affirmation of his knowledge of the proper and acceptable areas of interest to God. After all is said and done, we were/are simply created to act on His (God's) behalf or in His best interest. The Messianic Minister is the anointed representative of the Holy Spirit. Satan in his bid to deceive the masses has disguised himself as an "angel of light" and ordained his ministers as teachers of righteousness. These apostate ministers represent the apostate church. They would have you believe that God would eat from a table prepared by satan - a table wherefrom He would be served a meal of hog's guts, hog's head, pig feet, pig tails, hog brains and eggs, rump roast, cow's tongue, etc. - a meal certainly not in the interest of His good health. Take heed!

The Holy Ghost will soon provide the major challenge to the ministers of the apostate church as it causes the Holy Spirit to revive and strengthen the Messianic Ministry and Messianic Ministers. I admonish you to be circumspect when you go into the House of God.

For if it is truly the House of God, you will hear the servant conducting a service for God, promoting His interest. I am merely painting a picture for you of the world where you are, and guiding you unto the path that will lead you back unto God: the place where you need to be.

THE NEW (WORLD) ORDER

"Therefore my people are gone into captivity, because they have no knowledge; and their honorable men are famished, and their multitude dried up with thirst.

Therefore hell hath enlarged herself, and opened her mouth without measure; and their glory, and their multitude, and their pomp, and he that rejoiceth, shall descend into it."

Isaiah 5:13-14

"My people are destroyed for lack of knowledge; because thou hast rejected knowledge, I will also reject thee, that thou shalt be no priest to me; seeing thou hast forgotten the law of thy God, I will also forget thy children.

As they were increased, so they sinned against me; therefore will I change their glory into shame.

They eat up the sin of my people, and they set their heart on their iniquity."

Hosea 4:6-8

"How long shall I see the standard, and hear the sound of the trumpet?

For my people are foolish, they have not known me; they are stupid children, and they have no understanding; they are wise to do evil, but to do good they have no knowledge."

Jeremiah 4:21-22

"And though the Lord give you the bread of adversity, and the water of affliction, yet shall not thy teachers be removed into a corner any more, but thine eyes shall see thy teachers.

And thine ears shall hear a word behind thee, saying, This is the way, walk ye in it, when ye turn to the right hand, and when ye turn to the left."

Isaiah 30:20-21

"For the earth shall be filled with the knowledge of the glory of the Lord, as the waters cover the sea."

Habakkuk 2:14

The words of the prophets Isaiah and Habakkuk presage a time when we would bear witness to the pre-eminence of the knowledge of God. Daniel the Prophet also made direct mention of knowledge being increased at the end of Euro-gentile dominion. The adversary of God would have us direct our attention to the "accomplishments" of science and technology. While we are not naive about the temporal "progress" taking place, however, the primary point of Habakkuk's prophecy concerns the increase in the proliferation of truth at this time: the earth shall be full of the knowledge of the Lord as the waters cover the sea. During this epoch, the truth about God shall be easily discernible by even the simplest layman.

There is/shall be a resurgence of teachers that impart only comprehensible, undeniable truth. This unique period was predicted to coincide with the prophetic time entitled "Judgment Day." This particular Judgment Day does not initiate God's indignation toward the workers of iniquity. His wrath commenced with the sin of Adam and Eve, and His judgment has persistently assailed the human family, as a result of their misdeeds. This Judgment Day is different because it is eschatological (relating to the branch of theology concerned with the final events in the history of the world or mankind), signalling an end and a new beginning. Truth shall consume the lies as well as the liars that have filled the earth, terminate evil, and resurrect righteousness. Presently there is on-going spiritual warfare against deception, such as that seen in contemporary, apostate theological teachings which give the layman the false impression that at the consummate Judgment Day, he will be judged for all of his sins. The objective of these apostate teachings is to divert his attention from his present condition and cause him to focus on the days to come, rather than the time that is at hand.

Let us consider the dead and the judgment.

"And I saw the dead, small and great, stand before God, and the books were opened; and another book was opened, which is the book of life. And the dead were judged out of those things which were written in the books, according to their works.

And the sea gave up the dead that were in it, and death and hades delivered up the dead that were in them; and they were judged every man according to their works. And death and hades were cast into the lake of fire. This is the second death."

Revelations 20:12-14

As we peruse the written words of the revelation of John, keep in mind that God intended that we be guided by the words of His inspired prophets in obtaining a clearer understanding and making our final determination of the allegorical things that are described therein. It is necessary that I remind you again that judgment does not begin at terminal death, as we've been led to believe for so long, but actually began with the Edenic fall of Adam and Eve, and has continued, increasing in intensity as the centuries passed.

In considering matters of judgment, we must understand the prognostication of Ezekiel, the inspired prophet of God.

"But if the wicked will turn from all his sins that he hath committed, and keep all my statutes, and do that which is lawful and right, he shall surely live, he shall not die.

All his transgressions that he hath committed, they shall not be mentioned unto him: in his righteousness that he hath done he shall live.

Have I any pleasure at all that the wicked shall die? saith the Lord God: and not that he should return from his ways, and live?

But when the righteous turneth away from his righteousness, and committeth iniquity, and doeth according to all the abominations that the wicked man doeth, shall he live? All his righteousness that he hath done shall not be mentioned: in his trespass that he hath trespassed, and in his sin that he hath sinned, in them shall he die."

Ezekiel 18:21-24

Ezekiel gives us a very lucid understanding of judgment. He destroys our traditional Holy expectations about judgment and instead guides us to conclude that active judgment can only be executed while an individual is in control of a form of consciousness. In addition, there is but one complete end to consciousness, and that is to remain alienated from God, thus descending into the bottomless pit of the graveyard. However, anyone that maintains his God-mind merely undergoes a transfiguration and never completely loses his spiritual consciousness. This means that all resurrections and judgments of the sons of darkness (carnal-minded, opponents of God and what is right and holy) have to take place prior to their final death or loss of consciousness. Any resurrection or judgment after final descendancy would be useless. Ezekiel states that if a man consciously awakens and turns back unto God, none of his past would "be mentioned unto him;" only "in his righteousness shall he live," be seen or be judged. This individual would forever remain a conscious spirit even after his transfiguration. There is no need to resurrect him, for he shall never die; he has already been judged during his lifetime. He need not be resurrected from a graveyard to be told the consequences of his works, for Ezekiel has already informed him precisely where he stands. Prior, he needed only to believe the words of Ezekiel and hold fast to his faith and works for God.

To the contrary, he that consciously turns aside from God and chooses the world or mind of satan shall have none of his previous good works mentioned to him. Ezekiel warns that in iniquity shall he be judged, and none of his former "righteousness" shall be mentioned. There is no need to bring him back to consider his supposedly good works, for they are irrevelant.

> *"Ye adulterers and adulteresses, know ye not that the friendship of the world is enmity with God? Whosoever therefore will be a friend of the world is the enemy of God."*
>
> **James 4:4**

Accepting this prophetic truth allows us to properly determine that all resurrections and/or judgments are/can only take place during the season of consciousness. When those that have turned aside lose their final consciousness, they also lose their final choice. That places those individuals walking contrary to God in a very precarious predicament to say the least, for they have no promise of a tomorrow, and may lose that very tenuous last breath at any given moment. The devil stalks these fallen sons day and night trying to enhance the speed with which they shall arrive at their final destination. The devil prefers a loss of consciousness for if one retains consciousness, he may ultimately turn aside from him. It is for this reason that you've been endowed with an ample supply of consciousness-destroying "aid kits:" the sooner the loss of consciousness, the better. It is in this darkness that satan has structured the licentious social system. Remember, the fate of those who turn aside never changes as long as they remain alienated from God. One destiny awaits them. Their only hope is to be resurrected back unto God and life while they still possess consciousness.

Those that remain steadfast in God's service need not fear death for it can neither conquer nor overcome them. Their thoughts concerning

God's judgment are thus centered around the time they will be allowed to remain on this earth to develop or to be developed before being transformed into a carnate Holy Spirit. Thus, they may be summoned to another plane to be pressed into a higher service. Those that are alive in God but are not highly developed during this conscious lifetime will require more time to be further elevated for use in the higher realms as bearers of the power of the Holy Spirit. Therefore an extensive season may pass before his/her spirit is pressed into active service again. Remember all Holy Spirits are not in possession of the might and power, neither are they capable of being active in the day to day lives of the Saints. Of those that are active it is possible to feel their presense and spirit.

We have been thoroughly taught and warned from Genesis to James about the double-minded or "good and evil." James said the double minded should not expect to receive anything from God for they are unstable in all their ways. Even John the Revelator in his vision saw those that were double minded:

"I know thy works, that thou art neither cold nor hot; I would thou wert cold or hot.

So, then, because thou art lukewarm, and neither cold nor hot, I will spew thee out of my mouth."

Revelations 3:15-16

How does the hypocrite love God with all of his heart, soul and might? The image and will of God, the Father of your existence, was/is to be your only everlasting companion. You can have no interest in that of which God is not consulted or considered; there can be no portion of your existence that He cannot share. If God cannot share your life, He will not maintain it. To receive the fullness of life eternal requires you to be a full-time servant for God.

Eternal life is a priceless treasure; a most expensive pearl. Once you have acquired it, you agree to pay all that you have in your possession. Your life thus becomes God's light, and no man lights a candle and places it under a bushel or in hiding. Instead, it is placed where it may effectively give light unto all that are "on the Path." In the beginning it will take great courage to provide the light upon what will seem to be a lonely path with very few travellers. Nevertheless, your new life brings with it complete accountability unto God and compliance with His most Holy and Perfect Will.

Let us reflect upon the message of Lazarus and the rich man. While both of them maintained their consciousness, the impudent rich man chose extravagance while Lazarus chose God. In the metaphor (eyes) of God, the rich man's state of consciousness was seen as torment in hell, not as living. Lazarus, on the other hand, possessed a state of consciousness that conveyed the essence of life as God defined it, with no end, only higher planes. Thus, after completing one level of his conscious being, he merely continued on to a higher plane. Truthfully, therefore, Lazarus never died, and the evil rich man never lived, for he alienated himself from the Most High. The principal thing to remember here is that both men were judged during their conscious lifetimes. There will be no further judgment for the rich man. All that had to be said to him was said by Moses and the Prophets. Be assured therefore, that you will not enjoy or even have a chance to enjoy the new world or paradise except that you deny and break your allegiance to this world during your season of consciousness. Judgment Day will be in your conscious lifetime.

One of the great fabrications of satan is that there will be another judgment after physical death. His objective is/has always been to give you room to find comfort in maintaining your relationship with him. Subsequently he gives you the false impression that you may continue to serve him until you're without consciousness ("dead"), at which time the merciful God will resurrect you and possibly nullify the service you have paid satan. How could God possibly be the author of a doctrine which will/would allow you to murder, steal, lie, be licentious, worship the devil, commit whoredom, fornicate, etc., with the expectation that possibly everything will be alright when He considers your works after your physical death?

"O Lord our God, other lords beside thee have had dominion over us: but by thee only will we make mention of thy name.

They are dead, they shall not live; they are deceased, they shall

*not rise: therefore hast thou visited and destroyed them, and made
all their memory to perish."*

Isaiah 26:13-14

Even the foolish can understand that it is satan that has fostered such
erroneous teachings to keep you as active as possible on this earth in
his behalf. I am certainly aware that everyone's satanic involvement
is not to the same extent and degree. Not everyone in satan's parish
is an instructor; there are those that just love hearing what his teachers
have to say.

I firmly place the responsibility on the shoulders of every man by
giving him fair warning: there will be no judgment on the other side
of physical death. In other words, it is now or never. Every excuse
used to try to justify evil will only return to hurt the one that uses it.
Thus thou shall love the Lord God of Creation with all of thy heart,
all of thy soul and all of thy might. Pray to receive strength to
overcome all obstacles, express your desire to be his perfect servant.
Ask him to not overlook but correct even your secret faults. We can
only eradicate evil from this planet if we eradicate it from our lives.
Thus I admonish you: be not encouraged to do evil because it appears
that judgment is not executed speedily, for God doth try you to prove
what is in thy heart. Though a sinner do evil a hundred times and his
days be prolonged, hold fast to thy faith that it can/shall only be well
with those that fear Him and keep His commandments. The wicked
dieth in the bitterness of his soul, having never found pleasure before
God.

To further substantiate my exegesis concerning the resurrection and
judgment let us consider the events following the opening of the fifth
seal:

*"And when he had opened the fifth seal, I saw under the altar the
souls of them that were slain for the word of God, and for the
testimony which they held.*

*And they cried with a loud voice, saying, How long, O Lord, holy
and true, dost thou not judge and avenge our blood on them that
dwell on the earth?*

And white robes were given unto every one of them; and it was said unto them that they should rest yet for a little season until their fellow servants also and their brethren, that should be killed as they were, should be fulfilled. "

Here we are given a very enlightening picture of the whereabouts of those who maintained their God consciousness until the end of their work on this plane. These spirits are already around the throne discussing their return to active service as the avengers of the blood shed by the forces of evil. White robes were given to them and they were told to be patient, for their season had not yet come.

You may desire further discussion concerning the location of the altar and where those souls were going in their white robes. Nevertheless, we should be of one accord that they certainly were not in a graveyard waiting for resurrection and another judgment. I will touch upon the responsibility that has passed on to those patiently waiting in their white robes. Again we go to the vision of John.

He saw the high place called "heaven" opening up and those who had/have faith in the truth sitting upon a white horse. In righteousness they began to judge and make war. This no doubt is the eschatological judgment day when "The Word of God" becomes the King of kings and Lord of lords to lead the spiritual (celestial and terrestrial spirits) forces of God in the war against the political and ecclesiastical forces of evil (Euro-American/Euro-gentile). Those that were told to be patient at the opening of the fifth seal are now being pressed into service as part of the Host of Heaven.

"And the armies which were in heaven followed him upon white horses, clothed in fine linen, white and clean.

And out of his (their) mouth goeth a sharp sword (faith in truth - the Word of God becomes the weapon), *that with it he should smite the nations: and he shall rule them with a rod of iron* (strict order and firm discipline): *and he treadeth the winepress with the fierceness and wrath of Almighty God. "*

Revelation 19:14-15

65

"For Zion's sake will I not hold my peace and for Jerusalem's sake will I not rest, until her righteousness go forth as brightness, and her salvation as a lamp that burneth.

And the nations shall see thy righteousness, and all kings thy glory; and thou shalt be called by a new name, which the mouth of the Lord shall name.

Thou shalt also be a crown of glory in the hand of the Lord, and a royal diadem in the hand of thy God."

Isaiah 62:1-3

Judgment, or the relative recompense of humanity's works, has been propagating since the fall of Adam, which is evident from the continuous deterioration of real life and its infrastructure on this planet. There is a continuous rendering of judgment against "sinners" as a result of them not having the right knowledge of God, environment and self. Lies have ingratiated themselves with the leaders and people of this world. Consider an article in the December 18, 1990 issue of the Wall Street Journal entitled "Deadly Diet", in which Dr. Harold P. Freeman making his rounds at Harlem Hospital, stops at the bed of a patient suffering from high blood pressure and diabetes. Dr. Freeman is described lifting up the sheet to examine the woman's legs, so grotesquely swollen that they may have to be amputated. The doctor feels that her high fat, high salt diet of pig's feet and chitterlings, canned goods, fried foods, candy bars, soda, ice cream and pie has certainly contributed to her condition. "Do you think your diet is related to your condition?" the doctor asks. "No," she says, "It just happened to come on."

Judgment is upon her and countless others like her. Undoubtedly, their refrigerators are packed full to the brim with foods that are killing them. The destruction of lungs, livers, intestines and hearts, and the prevalence of cancers, herpes, V.D.'s and AIDS are all judgments that have cursed the people because of a lack of knowledge of the truth about God. Let us also consider the judgment for those trying to "better their lives" as recommended by the rulers of darkness.

Depo Provera is a hormone-based contraceptive injection manufactured by the Upjohn Company, and backed by the Food and Drug Administration (FDA). It is marketed in ninety (90) countries. It is administered by injection into the muscles at the back of the arm or in the buttocks, and must be re-administered every 90 days. The manufacturers of this contraceptive have been challenged for over twenty years concerning the drug's safety.

It is known that the drug's "side effects" cause women to experience: extreme weight gain, hair loss, heavy menstrual bleeding, irregular periods or no periods, abdominal pain, headaches, nervousness, dizziness, fatigue, and severe depression. These undesirable side-effects can persist for 6 - 10 months after the injection, and there is no immediate antidote. Regular pap smears must be stressed, because of the possible increased risk of cervical cancer.

African American women are at even extra risk because of their poor health status; thus they experience greater risk for breast cancer (which black women develop at younger ages than other women); greater depression (Afro-American women are rated as already living in psychological distress.) And if this isn't bad enough Afro-American women are already 45% obese, and additional weight gain can/will lead to increased rates of hypertension, kidney diseases and diabetes.

Despite these facts, the FDA says "this drug presents another long-term effective (though not safe) *option for women to prevent pregnancy." The National Planned Parenthood Federation of America, Inc. agreed.* (The macrocosmic underworld!)

**Excerpts from article entitled "Is Depo Provera Safe?" -
MS. Magazine, January/February 1993**

Man's mental state, which is almost always possessed by evil imaginations, certainly affects his physical well-being. The human family is trapped in the snares of death. The sorrows of hell compass them round about. The infinite wisdom of God's unquestionable judgment caused a condition to develop wherein there is a preponderance of people and institutions teaching that which is wrong. These individuals, although defined as having "higher education," have ensnared you to the point where you put your complete and utmost confidence in them. Subsequently you are taught ungodly knowledge that makes you support and partake of evil. That is the primary reason that people are being destroyed. They are being trained to pursue the vanities of this world, not to live.

Because of the continuous rejection of the message and messengers of God, our people and consequently all of humanity are victimized. God's messengers became fewer as His institutions were cast down while satan's emissaries and institutions multiplied. Due to this prophetic imbalance, you are exposed to the predominance of people and things that make you wiser to do what is wrong rather than those inclined to teach you to do what is right. This prepotency was of course in fulfillment of the Word and Will of God, allowing the curses to increase and your blessings to decrease. Universally, the people are continuously suffering because of a lack of basic knowledge and erudition about the God which created them. They have eyes which cannot see and ears which cannot hear, and stumble from the drunkenness of an overdose of false destructive doctrines. Nevertheless, the prophetic promise was made and shall find its fulfillment in these end-time days, the days of the Kingdom of God. Judgment Day for all false doctrine is when the desire for the glory of the knowledge of God surpasses that which exists for all other forms of knowledge.

This, little children, is the final hour, and the truth has to be told about life, death and the resurrection. You will soon know, whether accepted or not, that life is not, was not nor shall ever be in the abundance of your possessions. During his reign, the devil, is/was cognizant that he could never destroy the word of God (the Bible); he simply confused it and banished it, thus placing it in the realm of ineffectuality. Your mental and spiritual resurrection is the prerequisite to the revival of the effectiveness of the word of God. The adversary of God realized that in our redemptive struggle, we would need God on our side. He therefore hedged up the way to God with religion (the context in which you are taught to seek and find God) to ensnare you in your search. Now you are trapped. Consequently, when I say "God," you immediately think and relate as you've been taught: religiousity. Your misdirected instinct tells you that I'm trying to convert you to my or a new religion. This causes you to become defensive or fearful of my message, and just as satan has planned it, you close your ears to truths that will change your entire way of life.

So it is with most of the traditional concepts of your present religious beliefs, some of which are so obviously misleading. Let us consider for example, the contemporary supposition of the location of hell, which is relatively new as a geographical location. Hell owned no real estate in the beginning, nor was it necessary. Man's deviancy created a need for hell. Notwithstanding, it was never below the ground, only below heaven or down under heaven. From its inception, it has been on the face of the earth. The messengers of God clearly instructed us of its exact location: "The wicked shall be turned into hell, and all nations that forget God." The words "dig into her" as used by Amos the Prophet, could give a false impression of hell being beneath the soil. To dig down is metaphorically referring, in most instances as used by the prophets, as arriving at a place or a conclusion by way of deception, not with a shovel.

We find a similar reference to this subject by Samson, the thirteenth judge of the Children of Israel while being ruled by the Philistines. Shortly after Samson's marriage, he put forth a riddle to his guests and challenged them to find the answer within seven days or pay him a reward; if they would expound his riddle, they would be rewarded. They impressed upon his Philistine wife to seek out the answer and reveal it unto them, which she did. Upon them answering his riddle correctly, Samson was angered and responded to them: "If ye had not plowed (dug/dig) with my heifer, ye had not found out my riddle." (Judges 14:18) To plow is to dig up the soil or as meant by Samson: "if you had not worked deception on my woman (plowed with my heifer), you would not know my riddle."

How is it that satan has deceived the whole world and only a handful realize it? Except that evil has been institutionalized and made an acceptable standard, perversion, sexual explicity and decadence would not have a place in our lives. How have ungodly men, through religion, the media and all manner of commercially motivated activities deceived the people about God, life, death and the resurrection? To deceive is to cause to accept as true or valid that which is false and invalid; to lead astray; to mislead. Remember, a person who does not know when he is living, could not possibly understand when he is dying. If the adversary is to prevent the success of the Children of

God, he has to convince them that failure is success. How do men of evil design (workers of the devil) keep the Sons of God (God- fearing, righteous people) vilifying themselves? They have to convince decent people that ignorance (wearing clothing that's two- three sizes too large; wife swapping; indulging in cocaine and other drugs) is in fact intelligence or the "in thing." That is the essence of deception.

The fabric of your existence revolves, unfortunately, around materialism and perversions rather than the blessings of God. You're in pursuit of cars, homes, clothes, jobs and the like, believing all the while that these things determine success. You strive to attain them with all of your heart, soul and might. If your pursuit of God was in a like manner, you would have attained life everlasting plus all of the wealth imaginable from life's supporting infrastructure. Which do you consider true success: that which gives you a bank account or that which gives you life? Your false religion has taken you down from conduct to mere creed. You adhere to codes of conduct in all significant areas of society, sororities, clubs, fraternities, etc., but where God is concerned you have allowed someone to convince you that just "to believe" is sufficient. From Genesis to the Gospels, we've been taught and warned that our works shall determine our reward: what you reap is what you've sown.

"For the Son of man shall come in the glory of his Father with his angels; and then he shall reward every man according to his works."

Matthew 16:27

"But as touching the resurrection of the dead, have ye not read that which was spoken unto you by God, saying,

I am the God of Abraham, and the God of Isaac, and the God of Jacob? God is not the God of the dead, but of the living."

Matthew 22:31-32

"And another of his disciples said unto him, Lord, suffer me first to go and bury my father.

But Jesus said unto him, Follow me; and let the dead bury their dead."

Matthew 8:21-22

There is no rest for your souls, peace for your mind, health in your body, happiness in your family, nor the truth of God in your mind, and you've been convinced that it's all a part of life. Suffering is necessary, it is part of reality.

I am now pleading with you to understand that you've been deceived. For example, the above scriptures articulate for us the word death. Yeshua said God is the God of the living, not the dead. You don't need to be a genius to comprehend that He was not disclaiming His eminence over those in the cemeteries. He was making those who would hearken aware, that to die spiritually would cause them to lose their God. He was referring to the active dead, most of you that are turning these pages and reading these words. Reflect back over the words of the carpenter from Nazareth when approached by a disciple to attend a funeral: "Let the dead bury their dead." Here he clearly refers to a death that exists prior to the cemetery, or an end to a condition that already existed. The burial was actually the consummation of an evil process or existence, and to return to bury the dead body was vain; he felt that the ungodly could accomplish that. Nevertheless, Yeshua saw his contemporaries just as I see you: dead and without God.

God's adversary has to prevent His people from being reconciled unto Him. If God has separated Himself from the spiritually dead, the devil's objective is to perpetuate their state of unconsciousness. Satan knows that if you were conscious of your actual predicament, you'd change, therefore he has to prevent your comprehension of the truth about your situation. He has you thinking that you're really living, just as those who were spiritually dead thought as they buried their dead. It is pertinent to understand that the concept of "resurrection" in the High, Holy and Sacred language of Hebrew (used by the inspired Prophets and Messengers of God) is preserved as a pure basic idea. Their expression of this concept, (תחיית המתים) "tikheeyat hamateem" is figuratively "coming back to life from the dead." This

71

simply means that there will be a restoration to life from the dead. The deception is concerning the type of rebirth, i.e. a restoration from a spiritual versus carnal death. With the help of the God of Israel's guiding light, I will make the way straight.

I realize that it is not possible to immediately remove the myth or the mystery surrounding everlasting life. Therefore, my objective is merely to return everlasting life to its original intent, thereby making it attainable. If I accomplish this, my effort will not have been in vain. Soon, the great majority of the earth's inhabitants will have to admit that they are not created in the image and after the likeness of God. The first man Adam fell, and his Godly image was replaced by an ungodly similitude. Maintaining the God image and life without the breath (rendered נשמה in Hebrew, pronounced "neshama") of life actively providing the direction isn't possible. The soul is only considered alive if this special life force is breathed into it; only that makes a human truly human. It is what distinguishes man from beast. Mankind must have the spiritual element of/or God within him in order to be a real man. God's purpose for putting the "neshama" into Adam was to transform him into His servant, active only on His behalf. Subsequently he was required to perform for or as God, to function only within a Divinely-prescribed course of activity and within a limited environment. Contemporary science declares the existence of mankind extends millions of years prior to Adam. However, if there were those that preceded this new Adam, God's objective was that Adam reflect the intervention of God's presence into the affairs of man. Along with the appearance of Adam, order was manifested.

Truthfully you/we must establish order to conquer disorder. It is only after order is established that disorder can be identified, challenged and corrected. Satan always prefers disorder because it hides and protects his presence. Everything is negatively affected by disorder. Where there is no order in the family there can never be true joy as prescribed by God; when disorder reigns, humanity suffers. It is the indefiniteness of manhood, womanhood and childhood as defined by the Euro-American culture that has caused the chaotic condition upon the planet today. To appreciate this fully, you must realize that indefiniteness denotes the absence of stability and reason. In disorder everyone and everything can be defined as God, life, love and living. However, such vagueness very subtly denies the existence of God and order.

> *"Higher ideas and a better way of life cannot be properly defined (nor appreciated) unless one has a contrasting flourishing manifestation of the progress achieved outside the confines of existing society. One can never totally realize the effects of homosexuality in the community or nation until one finds a community free of it and its corruption.*
>
> *Nor can one speak authoritatively on the issues and benefits of establishing communities emphasizing moral values and founded on the principles and laws of God unless one has found an example of a redeemed people, progressively expanding and excelling through adherence to the laws and statutes of God..."*
>
> **<u>God the Black Man and Truth</u>**
> **by Ben Ammi, Communicators Press**

The American political hierarchy is a fitting example of what I mean. The system fluctuates between Democrats and Republicans, liberals and conservatives. The Supreme Court receives its appointees in this same manner. Consequently, over the years issues such as homosexuality, abortion and the banning of school prayer have alternately become acceptable or not acceptable, right or wrong, good or evil. Society overall is greatly affected by this state of indefiniteness. As a result, the disorder in our society leaves the people with the erroneous impression that it is merely "a matter of preference", as in whether to eat an orange or a grapefruit. This confusion in the social system allows for the creation of every evil work. The revelation of John confirms:

> *"And after these things I saw another angel come down from Heaven..."*
>
> *And he cried mightily with a strong voice, saying, Babylon the Great* (Euro-American/Euro-gentile democratic social systems) *is fallen, is fallen, and is become the habitation of devils, and the*

hold of every foul spirit and a cage of every unclean and hateful bird."

Revelations 18:1-2

Order and definity are the necessary keys to bring an end to the prevailing disorder of satanic dominance over man's conscious existence. The coming of the Kingdom of God signals the beginning of the end. It was Daniel, the inspired prophet of God, who forecast the establishing of the Kingdom of God during the final reign of Euro-Gentile world supremacy embodied in the (European Common Market). This economic super power would succeed in the <u>deification</u> of money. All of the earth's inhabitants have drowned themselves in the pursuit of this god and the things it can purchase for them. With this new god, they feel they can do anything; without it, they can do nothing. They work for, labor for, toil for (worship), <u>the Almighty Dollar</u>. Money is sought after as the primary source of life on this planet, supplanting the God of creation.

The pursuit of this paper god is the cause of ninety percent of crime world wide. The people live by the dollar, suffer because of the dollar, are killed or die prematurely - all because of the dollar, yen, sterling, franc, or the mark. This economic force has caused a great flood of corruption to both people and the planet. Because of this unparalleled iniquity, love in this world has waxed cold, having lost her place to the strong burning desire for vanity.

This Holy Kingdom at its inception was to exist parallel with this economic super power as a mirror reflection of those nations. The coming of The Kingdom, therefore, identifies the spirit that governs them and signals the season of their demise. It is the same corresponding message with the rise of Jacob and the fall of Esau and Yeshua's statement that the gospel of the kingdom presages the end of this evil age.

"The earth mourneth and fadeth away, the haughty people of the earth do languish.

The earth also is defiled under the inhabitants thereof; because they have transgressed the laws, changed the ordinance, broken the everlasting covenant."

Isaiah 24:4-5

Thus we conclude that the true genesis began with the establishment of order into the life of Adam, from which we were to draw our conclusions and begin our journey. Without the God-mind, we are human in body only, but it's our actions that distinguish us from one another. Man, without the God presence, is only man in shape and form, but in mind or character is actually base, animalistic, a lower form in the realm of the creations. The attributes of the God-mind -- intelligence, instinct, discernment etc. -- are precisely for maintaining the creations and man himself, but after his alienation from God, man's intelligence and instincts were used for wicked and mischievous ends.

Man today has fallen so low that presently he procreates "in the image" and after the likeness of satan, God's arch adversary rather than after God. It is evident in practically all aspects of society today, that evil in the form of illicit sex, violence, death and destruction are the norm rather than looked upon as perverse and abnormal. How can we view teenage unwed parenthood, rampant drug use and astronomical crime waves in cities across the planet, as God-like behaviour? However, the resurrected sons and daughters of God have returned to the genesis and are again creating in the image and likeness of God. With their resurgence, teachers of righteousness have been born to inform you that there has to be a new beginning, a new creation, new images, the return of Godly images and standards of beauty and joy. Only when God's spirit (sense) is renewed in you shall you know the joy and gladness of salvation and come to fully appreciate the blessings of God.

All of God's people living in Euro-gentile dominated social systems are considered to be dwelling under the shadow of death. Death is everywhere; society has gone mad. The acceptance of sin is condoned and promulgated in our society's institutions, which are controlled and governed by evil, devil-inspired men. By disguising himself as an "angel of light", satan manipulated his way into the seats of government and authority. Under his influence governments legislate policies and pass laws that have exculpated evil, in order to maintain satan's presence and/or influence and dominion. The sad part is, people are oblivious to this evil-ruled world of death, destruction, poverty, fear, anxiety, pollution, perversion, degeneracy, disrespect, immorality, plagues, sickness and disease. This abnormal state of existence is considered normal. This testifies that evil concepts, systems of government and implementation devices have been established for and accepted entirely by the people as correct and normal, thus solidifying satan's control. Everyone is afraid to buck the system, or status quo, for fear of jeopardizing their personal status (jobs, standing in the community) in his evil society. The aftermath of this complacency and fence straddling (going to church and saying "I believe" on Sunday, then doing whatever you want the rest of the week) will be paid for with their souls and the souls of future generations.

> *"The people that walked in darkness have seen a great light: they that dwell in the land of the shadow of death, upon them hath the light shined."*
>
> **Isaiah 9:2**

> *"But judgment shall return unto righteousness: and all the upright in heart shall follow it.*
>
> *Who will rise up for me against the evildoers? or who will stand up for me against the workers of iniquity?"*
>
> **Psalms 94:15-16**

Everlasting life has but one enemy - death. Death is the most feared negative force of the creation. Yet he has the largest number of followers of any philosophy upon the planet earth! He is dreadful, unpleasant, and abhorringly ugly. Yet the earth's inhabitants cleave to him and take him with them everywhere they go. If this be the case, the mystery is why is everyone attracted to him? The answer is simple: they can't see him! When the blind leads the blind, they both fall in the ditch. Furthermore, only the living know the dead. They, only, have eyes to see him (the devil).

Spiritual death is the separation of man from God. With the death of the all-powerful "God Mind", man's understanding of the Plan of God is lost. Also with it is lost his understanding of its relationship to him. Spiritual or mental death is the first step towards eternal damnation. It is the inevitable result of being disobedient to the Plan of God.

We find in the beginning that God instructed Adam: "I have given you every herb-bearing seed which is upon the face of all the earth, and every tree, in them which is the fruit of a tree-yielding seed. This shall be the nourishment for your soul. Also, you may eat (listen) freely of every tree that is of the garden except the tree with the doctrine of good and evil. These trees shall provide your spiritual (mental) nourishment. In the day that the spirit of disobedience is allowed to destabilize your thinking, an appalling change in your attitude, coupled with your actions toward Me will manifest and unveil your nakedness (lack of my spirit within you)." The guilt hidden in darkness in his soul shatters his inward peace and destroys his sense of companionship with the Beloved One who had freely given him all things in abundance. No wealth of the world can then compare with the wealth lost by turning aside from his creator.

Sin against the Plan of God causes complete mental insanity as Adam (man) hides himself from the presence of God or attempts to deny the truth of God's teachings. He becomes hardened inwardly, and thus does not allow the blood of life to pass smoothly through his arteries and veins. You will see an outward change - obscurity and pre-mature aging - as the spiritual death occurs, and the loss of the smooth softness and beauty of a living, radiant body. When you're alive, you are light, mobile and vibrant, both physically and mentally.

Motion is life-giving, therefore it is perpetual. There are three main areas of concentration: mind in motion means learning is perpetual. The brain motion is study, learning. When an individual is between the tender age of fifty to seventy (50-70) years, he/she should be involved in intense study. Not only should they be deeply involved with the learning process, but they should be in pursuit of the more complex studies or subjects. Comparatively speaking, those between the ages of five and twenty-five, except in rare occasions, are not even capable of applying themselves to a fifty year old's level of serious study. In addtion, after three to five years away from formal study, all individuals should return to the classroom as a teacher or student.

Study to the mind is proper nourishment. At no time can it be discontinued. When an individual ceases to study or partake in a serious learning process, he is literally destroying his mind. Most elders have simply been programmed to become senile and sedentary. They are encouraged to do nothing, think about nothing serious and "retire" from meaningful pursuits in life. It is not uncommon to find instances where individuals, after having conducted mentally challenging and vigorous lifestyles, have died suddenly and unexplainedly shortly after retirement. Literally, they had nothing left to live for. They are prompted along this path by allowing themselves to become estranged from the laws of God that govern all living. The second is motion of body, physical activity, exercise that challenges. Challenging physical activity is forever. The last is motion of direction, that is accomplished through vision, objectives, aspirations. You should always have an objective that when attained, will bring you a form of satisfaction, a sense of accomplishment. Aspirations kindle inspiration to live. Do you remember the familiar statement: "This is my goal in life!"?

When you're dead, you are heavy, immobile and dull. God gave us an assiduous plan for our way of life, with an unlimited ability to learn His ways. In contrast, a social system that derides or subtly limits the desire to walk, run and play, alienates you from sunshine, moonlight and fresh air and places you in a state of deactivation, is leading you to decadence and degeneracy. This world deprives its inhabitants of the very essentials of life while overloading them (their hearts) with the desire to pursue vanities, diverting their attention from the life-giving relevance of God and Holiness. Even when good things come into the presence of a fool, the end result will be evil. The animalistic (lower form of intelligence) acts of sexual deviants (homosexuals, hermaphrodites, pedophiliacs, necrophiliacs, transvestites, etc.), stem from a lack of understanding, not intelligence. They literally don't know what to do with themselves. Their mental faculties are underdeveloped. This is illustrated in the expressions of disco, punk rock and drug cultures, bikini bathing suits, mini dresses and see-through blouses. These expressions are not creations of a vibrant mind.

The past times of smoking, consuming destructive strong drink and wife exchanging show a lack of creative genius. Even modern medicine, radio and television, transportation and education were good at their conception, but were made evil by stagnant minds. The devil's constituents are stationed hours before the television, only breaking to check their batteries in their computers. Afterwards they drive to the corner store to shop for ready-cooked foods with warming instructions on the label for their microwave oven. Everything is geared to a people with no time: that don't know how to cook, eat, to spend their earnings, nor enjoy the pleasure of people. All of their time has been taken away. Time is immortal, and is required in order to live. It in itself is life. Death is when time is taken away. But satan, the master deceiver, made you think that the microwave, faster cars, computers and other inventions would give you more time. In a dead society there is no time to walk, no time to cook, no time to eat, no time to digest. In the course of a worldly day, there is absolutely no time to live. You cannot move yourselves; only the Word of God can enliven you. "Come unto me all ye that are heavy laden, and I will give you life for your souls."

"Then Peter said, Lo, we have left all, and followed thee.

And he said unto them, Verily I say unto you, There is no man that hath left house, or parents, or brethren, or wife, or children, for the kingdom of God's sake,

Who shall not receive manifold more in this present time, and in the age to come life everlasting."

Luke 18:28-30

To hide one's self from the source of life, (the light of God), will indeed bring on death. Once spiritual (mental) death is accomplished, bodily death and the death of the soul is inevitable. The level of

God-consciousness required to maintain a living body and soul dete-riorates. The soul is the inner organisms of the physical body of man. Its relationship to the spirit is inseparable; it was created as the dwelling place of the Holy Spirit, the manifestor and perpetuator of its existence. The soul without the Spirit of God will die/is dead.

The Spirit of God is accompanied by the natural law of instinct. Instinct is not really imbued into the impulse or faculty of man's psyche. It exists infinitely within the cycles of life and is manifested by the spirit. Instinct guides and directs by Divine intellect and inclination. It protects and shields against dangers unknown or un-seen. Without pre-instruction or teachers, it directs men to walk in the proper direction, eat the correct foods, and speak the right words.

When the spirit enters into its temple or dwelling place, it brings relative laws (instructions) necessary to maintain a perpetual exist-ence. Law is required to assure the life presence in the soul of man. The law of relativity molds for us the fundamental knowledge of food that is good for consumption. We find the mention of food for physical utilization very early in the scriptures. We are instructed concerning the proper diet to maintain a living soul. No doubt you've sometimes wondered why the concentration on nutrition comes so soon after the spiritual (mental) awakening. There is a law that governs the living spirit's occupancy. First it enters in, then it prepares for itself a Holy habitation. Numerous writers and teachers have also brought to our attention that the inner physical body (soul) is the temple of God. We know that in former times the temple was considered the central area for the worship of God. In our earlier writings we have clarified that worship is to work for, labor for, toil for God. With that under-standing, we can see the correlation between the words "temple" and "worship." That is to say, that the soul (temple) would be the center or the focal point of all the activities, or the continuous actions done on behalf of God. Authors and masters of old that touched upon these things were trying to steer the people back to God by using similitudes.

They referred to the temple of God being within you, attempting to draw a comparison between their understanding of the structural temple and the soul temple. Needless to say, the people did not understand. Even today, they do not understand that when the mind dies, the activities or works (worship) for God soon cease. Then, as the God activities cease, the satanic activities (devil worship) certainly begin. The victim becomes a moving corpse destined for the cemetery.

In the Qumran Community's* dissertations on flesh and spirit, the initial message concerned the bondage of doing what is right when you have no spirit. The fact is, when the spirit is present, to do what is right is relatively easy - a righteous spirit is full of joy, love, goodness, faith, peace of mind, etc. The true justification for any action stems from an internal spiritual conviction (the soul being motivated by God or manipulated by satan), not the letter of the law (ritualistic practice). To comply with the law perfectly without inner faith or spirit is to no avail. No man can be justified by the works of the law without the spirit or inner convictions. In the flesh you are motivated by a desire to be seen. From the soul/spirit you are motivated by a desire to live in harmony with the will of God. Therefore do not keep the outward law of the flesh, but the spiritual law of the soul. Yeshua realized during his ministry that the Law had become only an outward expression of the flesh, but inwardly they were likened unto "whited sepulchers" (graves or tombs). All of those who come now must keep the law of the spirit, not the flesh. Eventually we must return to Genesis and our natural righteous instinct.

"And be not conformed to this world: but be ye transformed by the renewing of your mind, that ye may prove what is that good, and acceptable, and perfect, will of God."

Romans 12:2

The spirit is nourished by Divine and Holy thoughts. The soul is nourished by Divine and Holy diet. They are inseparable. The Living Spirit (resurrected) will then resurrect the body's perfect worship of God (laboring for, toiling for, all actions for and in harmony with God's creation), collectively creating a rejuvenated body. This is the

---

Contemporary historians assert that both Paul and Yeshua were members of this sect of Israelites, the former having betrayed them and interpolated their teachings.

81

second resurrection. We now see spiritual discipline moving to cause physical discipline. These two disciplines combine to cause the third resurrection: the resurgence of the soul, vigor, vitality and the power to endure, completing the cycle and causing man to experience absolute life.

Maintaining the three disciplines - of spirit (mind), body and soul - will lock you in cycle or bring you to what the prophets called "everlasting life," which is simply a state of existence without death. I will not try to explain everlasting life in terms of years, although we can use 969 years (Methuselah's age) for the sake of discussion. We know that in years, it can be at least that. But in truth, we must know that everlasting life is merely our lives or existence without the presence of death. When the undisciplined, do-as-I-please, evil spirit of death is destroyed, all people will come into the time of eternal life.

So now as we continue to unlock the mysteries and make the way straight, we will meet the realities of life and death head on. We shall not know the reward of everlasting life by the number of years, but the principal thing we will know is how to attain it - by gaining the victory over death. There from, whatever we receive will only be known as we share that experience.

"I would like you to join me on a journey of discovery. We will explore a place where the rules of everyday existence do not apply. These rules explicitly state that to grow old, become frail, and die is the ultimate destiny of all. And so it has been for century after century. However, I want you to suspend your assumptions about what we call reality so that we can become pioneers in a land where youthful vigor, renewal, creativity, joy, fulfillment, and timelessness are common experiences of everyday life, where old age, senility, infirmity, and death do not exist and are not even entertained as a possibility.

If there is such a place, what is preventing us from going there? It is not some dark continental land mass or dangerous uncharted sea. It is our conditioning, our current collective world view that we were taught by our parents, teachers, and society. This way of seeing things - the old paradigm - has aptly been called 'the hypnosis of social conditioning' an induced fiction in which we have collectively agreed to participate.

Your body is aging beyond your control because it has been pro-

grammed to live out the rules of that collective conditioning. If there is anything natural and inevitable about the aging process, it cannot be known until the chains of our old beliefs are broken."

Ageless Body, Timeless Mind by Deepak Chopra, M.D.,
Harmony Books, New York, 1993

Those that continue under the influence of God will be blessed to live in a place called Heaven, in surroundings called "Paradise." All of these, my children, are attributes used to describe the good things of God, which are called "Blessings." Has not the Father said "eyes have not seen and ears have not heard" what the reward will be for those who attain "Everlasting Life"?

After the Divine warning to Adam, recorded in the second chapter of Genesis, Adam disobeys God's instructions concerning the trees and warning of a subsequent fall. The first pronouncement by God announces Adam's death to occur on the very day of his insubordination. This death is his separation (mentally and spiritually) from God as a result of his defiance of the Plan of God. Following the mental separation (death), we find the next pronouncement to be the inevitable Second Death: the death of the body. "Who told thee that thou was naked? Has thou eaten of the tree whereof I commanded thee that thou shouldest not eat?" This was soon followed by the death of the soul (internal organic deterioration), as God states "cursed to the ground" and the produce it shall yield unto you. All the remaining days will be for the continuous destruction of your physical well-being. Certainly we must know that this statement could only be referring to the inevitable Third Death, since the first and second had already occurred. The third separation is now set in motion from the first and second - the separation of man's mind and body (works/worship) from the spirit or intellect of God, which was for his well-being, and then the separation of nature from man, which was to provide for his organic well-being.

We can certainly attest that the ground is cursed. Just peep into the hallways of clinics, hospitals and waiting rooms of private physicians. Nevertheless, satan must prevent you knowing that the food you consume is grossly laced with all types of chemicals, preservatives and carcinogens. Even if you do know, he'll cause you not to care, seducing you with catchy jingles and laughing faces to entice you to buy regardless of the food's poisonous contents. Satan must deny the revelation of truth to his already spiritually dead subjects. Thus, though he could not bring forth food for life and health, he could deceive the carnal eye by filling the supermarket shelves with his chemically-produced products that look like the originals. (Satan is a master imitator.) Of course, you eat them until they absolutely kill you. By the way, your plot awaits you in the local cemetery, the place they bury those that partake of the consequential third death.

It was not always called a cemetery; nor did it exist in the early days of the creation. The people had not yet come into the fullness of dreadful satanic death (godless-spiritless body). Preceding the time of the "cemetery," the burial area was called מנוח בית a "Bait Manoak," or חיים בית "Bait Kiyeem," translated as "the habitation of rest," or "House of Life." Together with that, our fathers knew the reward of death, for they always closed with the words "may his soul rest in peace." Although there are some ministers that still use those words, they are not conscious of the spiritual significance of this statement. Statements of this sort are a paradigm that our people used to describe the great hardships and burdens placed upon them by this world. They felt that peace and rest could only be attained by getting out, or, leaving it. The fact is that due to a lack of knowledge, they were not able to draw the proper conclusion and thereafter attain the rest and peace they sought through a mental (spiritual) rebirth (resurrection) into another world. They could only relate somewhat superficially to the need to die as a prerequisite to attain rest for their souls that were weary from the hard bondage and enter the house of life or the habitation of the living to inherit the new world or paradise. At this point I would be remiss if I not touch upon the truth and the myth surrounding "dying and going to Heaven."

"Few will deny that the white spiritual was primarily and almost exclusively other-worldly. Its creators were people who looked beyond the troubles and disappointments, even the partial success (such as being white), of this life and yearned for the perfections of heaven. True and complete salvation was in their every thought. Because their religion was

a compartment in their lives, a kind of Sunday exultation, instead of the whole thing, they could afford this kind of preoccupation. Because they were lacking in a long and deep religious tradition as well as a song tradition, they had had little practice matching artistic symbols with the affairs of everyday life. They stuck to raw, simple, desperate expressions of hope for themselves as individuals in the great beyond.

With the Negro creator almost everything was the opposite. His traditions in song and wholehearted religion were deep enough, his everyday life was hard and brutal and to him unjust enough, his use of mask and symbol was skillful enough, his faith in earthly future was intense enough that he could sing of his earthly life and do it artistically. In any case he sang of this earth, as many thoughtful students and observers have testified."

**Black Song: The Forge and the Flame, by John Lovell, Jr.
Paragon House Publishers, New York 1986**

The true understanding of the Biblical prophetic exhortation to "die and go to Heaven" is adverse to what is being promulgated intensely through religion today. The force of evil knew full well from the Adamic experience that the fallen Sons would have to die again in order to inherit Paradise. As generations passed, erudition deteriorated, leaving behind a more mundane understanding of the redemptive prophetic message. The Euro-gentile interpolators subsequently seized the power to define and reinterpreted the once-attainable "Heaven" as being in a far off distant space in an unknown location (presumably somewhere in the sky in one of God's galaxies), unreachable and inexplicable. Once the contemporary phalanx of religious interests was given the reins, they expanded the realms of deception, using good and evil (half truths). They formulated your thought pattern on an incomplete sentence structure: "You must die and go to Heaven," sufficiently fulfilling satan's objective. The adversary, realizing the limitations of people's understanding, capitalized on this ineptness, and deceived them to think that his prescribed death would fulfill their expectations. Remember, deception's power is in convincing you that what is wrong is right. The objective was, is and always will be to create an aloof indifference about true life and good health. This is easily understandable, for it was not their charge to make you aware that dying refers/referred simply to their world and being resurrected into a new, higher form of life or Heaven. As you "died" to God in Genesis, and lost your Heavenly possessions, you were/are being exhorted to "die" to the world of satan, the prerequisite for going to Heaven or another world, both here on this planet. With your good and evil satanic awakening, you died to God's world and went down into the depths of hell. Now judgment requires that you change and forsake this world of compounded evil, that you may be received again in your former Heavenly estate. The following pages will give further clarity on this subject.

Taking advantage of your missing God-intellect, satan runs roughshod over your stagnant, unresponsive minds, knowing of your inability to consciously discern his evil ways and systems. Satan has been served well by your failure to detect his Genesis character. This in itself is a testimony of the power of deception. As a rule we were all deceived by the prevalent religious institutions wherein we were taught to perceive satan as a force of compounded evil. Even <u>Webster's Universal Dictionary</u> defines satan as "the great enemy of man and goodness." However, not once have I heard anyone expounding on the exceedingly cunning, deceptive, and very subtle "good works" of satan. Someone purposely caused us to be led astray from the message of Genesis: satan was/is a tree of <u>good</u> and <u>evil</u>.

I recall hearing with great regularity in my childhood "Son, just look for the good in people" and "Son, everyone has some good in them." Little did I know and less did I understand how accurate these statements were. My parents continuously brought people home that had "some" good in them. When I inquired as to why they had a tail, a pitchfork and horns, they would tell me "Now don't be hard-headed; everyone has some good in them." It is certainly evident to me now that this is how satan has deceived the whole world. He uses his good to gain access for a moment in order to proliferate his evil for an hour. That is to say that his good is not the good of conviction but of strategy, a strategy used to make inroads for evil: good deeds with an evil motive. This is the spirit that has protected satan since his inception. The good in him has prevented him from being apprehended and convicted, and thus allows his evil to continue the unabated destruction of this planet.

The provenance and connection between the aforementioned and most of the social ills that befall man today, find their roots in the constitutions governing Euro-American/Euro-gentile countries. These constitutions are the epitome of good and evil government. You are given the freedom to worship the God of creation or satan; free to print the truth or the lie; free to influence rightly or wrongly. This form of government is compelled to protect and serve the interest of both good and evil. In sharp contrast to governments under the influence of err, the Kingdom of God has been instructed to pursue a social system based upon good and right and to love the God of Israel with all of our hearts, souls and might, serving His interests and His alone. Can you imagine dispatching God's Army to protect the rights of devil worshippers? A house divided against itself cannot stand!

The insidious dual nature of satan has made him undetectable, ofttimes even invisible because no one knew that satan had any good in him. Whenever his evil arouses suspicion, he reverts to some strategic good... for a while. He thus removes the tension while he simultaneously solicits praise: "How could he possibly be the devil and do all of those good works?" He that is of my flock can hear my voice.

In order to fortify his dominion over the minds of the dead, he continues to strengthen his position. He shares with you his cunning skills for duplicating his immoral acts; he rewards his subjects with inanimate benefits. Then you boastfully come forth; you are so proud he has given you so much of what was once all his. Of course he didn't just volunteer those devilish skills; you insisted that he give you an equal opportunity to be a little devil. For without his training, you would not be able to do your portion in destroying man and nature.

I must admit, you are now holding your own at Monsanto, Dupont, Upjohn Company, Ford, Standard Oil and the like. No doubt you can now make napalm and agent orange all by yourself. You now run a dead heat with satan. He can depend upon you to make the deadline for him, for he has trained you to be dead right. Then he feeds you poisons all day, everyday. You read it on the labels and laugh yourself to hell. At the conclusion of the matter, it is as Yeshua of Nazareth once said, they take you out in your fine, expensive casket in your best (sometimes new) suit, the final act of grandeur as "the dead bury the dead."

Today's incapacitated humanoid uses only 10% of his brain capacity. This is significant when noting that he also lives only 10% or less the years of the fallen Edenic man. Comparing Adam's life, we find in Genesis after the birth of Seth, Adam lived (his physical body) eight hundred years, begetting sons and daughters. He continued on for a total of nine hundred and thirty years. He continued to exist in an environment which was in relative harmony with God. He had to toil for hundreds of years to destroy his physical body. Of course things have changed since then. Not having time to toil like Adam, you have created chemicals for yourself to accomplish the job in less than one-tenth of that time. You don't have to linger around that long trying to destroy your health. You've become an expert at self-destruction. You've also fixed your environment so that you get maximum assistance from it. As a matter of fact, you use everything you get your hands on. Adam didn't have access to your science and technology. It took him so long to destroy his soul, whereas now you jump out of the womb fighting against life. You're Carnation babies... of course!

THE EVIL SPIRITS THAT VIE FOR THE SOULS OF MEN

It is not my objective to dwell extensively on diet in my dissertation on everlasting life, for there are many excellent writings on the subject. I will mainly relate to issues which serve as the determining factors as to whether any dietary program will be effective. One seeking rejuvenation through diet must first seek rejuvenation of spirit - a renewing of his relationship with God Almighty. Without this reconciliation, the benefits will only be minimal, sufficiently deceptive to give the impression of progress.

We must pursue change through spiritual enlightenment and physical deeds as we are taught by God and guided by His prophets and prophecies. Reposing in God's word we shall see a direct connection between the two worlds - spiritual and physical - hearing, thinking and doing. External human behavior has a direct influence upon the functioning of both the internal organs of the soul and the universal forces. I am sure that the spread of AIDS began with hearing the words "promiscuity is fun and innocuous," giving the impression that an evil lifestyle would not result in the production of evil in other areas, as if to say there is no nexus between the spiritual and physical.

The laws of spiritual purity are not just for your spirit, but for your physical well-being as well, to prevent the defilement, abuse and abasement of yourself, your people and the creations of God.

It is important for you to realize the direct correlation between the spiritual and physical being. In order to truly live and succeed in life, you must fully appreciate the relationship between psychology and physiology. It's not enough to eat correctly and consume vitamins and minerals; your spiritual expression determines your physical condition. Too often we hear about avid health or physical fitness fanatics falling ill or dying at an early age. It is this kind of occurrence which gives health food and exercise a bad reputation. But truthfully, these "health advocates" have most likely focused exclusively on their physical beings and neglected their spiritual God-minds. When an individual of the underworld (the world beneath/hell) consumes his salad and drinks his carrot juice, he receives results which are commensurate with his relationship with God or satan. It matters not that a son of darkness will no doubt use the charts or statistics of his world, which will accordingly give the impression of benefits. He has never lived in another realm, but will accept worldly reasoning, and become complacent toward change. The rewards of consuming salad and carrot juice as received by someone who has a spirit which is in harmony with God are totally different from those received by someone with no Godly spirit. Everything has to agree: no benefits of God under satan, and no benefits of satan under God.

It is only the objective of the Eternal to give you life more abundant, and on to everlasting life. The Creator has clearly emphasized that He is the God of the Living. Only the Most High is truthfully interested in giving you peace of mind and health of body. All other forces are to merely create an illusion of peace, life and health. Thus, it is my objective to make you cognizant of the delusion and the lie; then to sprinkle clean water (doctrine/truth) upon you, thereby giving you a new birth under God. This new spirit will cause you to walk in His statutes and be obedient to His instructions. No mind can serve two masters, for either it will hate the one and love the other; or else it will hold to the one and despise the other. A double mind is unstable unto God in all of its ways. For thou must love the Lord thy God with all of your heart, all of your soul and all of your might. The new birth begins with the realization that there has to be absolute change in your lives; no new wine in old bottles, no new cloth on an old garment. The message is explicitly clear: cosmetic change will not be sufficient. The new birth will lift you up out of the world of contemporary Greco-Roman theological mythology, allowing you the eternal blessing of once again understanding truth.

Truth is the uncompromising enemy of deception; no matter how vehemently denied, it cannot be changed. In these times of great adversity, sottishness and evident hopelessness, the failure of traditional religions to produce positive results is a needless argument with a serious-minded individual. Be not deceived! Humanity has to unite and build a new world governed by men governed by God, or accept eternal damnation in this present one ruled by the spirit in opposition to God. The decisions that confront our generations are in most cases not easy ones, but they are the decisions that will determine if the coming generations will have a place on this planet earth. There has to be a revolution, inspired by the desire to do right and the vision of a righteous world. Only through a new birth will you be able to comprehensively see the truth to which I refer throughout these writings. The reader is admonished to study carefully the things written herein and pray for understanding. No longer must God's word be viewed with skepticism; you can't afford to make the wrong decision. In these exceedingly evil times, it is your choice of being eternally blessed or cursed.

"For all the prophets and the law prophesied until John.

And if ye will receive it, this is Elijah, which was to come.

He that hath ears to hear, let him hear."

Matthew 11:13-15

"And his disciples asked him, saying, Why then say the scribes that Elijah must first come?

And Jesus answered and said unto them, Elijah truly shall first come, and restore all things.

91

But I say unto you, That Elijah is come already, and they knew him not, but have done unto him whatsoever they listed. Likewise shall also the Son of man suffer of them.

Then the disciples understood that he spake unto them of John the Baptist."

Matthew 17:10-13

"When Jesus came into the coasts of Caesarea he asked his disciples, saying, Whom do men say that I the Son of man am?

And they said, Some say that thou art John the Baptist: some, Elijah; and others, Jeremiah, or one of the prophets.

He saith unto them, But whom say ye that I am?

And Simon Peter answered and said, Thou art the Christ, the Son of the Living God.

And Jesus answered and said unto him, Blessed art thou, Simon Bar-jona: for flesh and blood hath not revealed it unto thee, but my Father which is in heaven."

Matthew 16:13-17

"At that time Herod the tetrarch heard of the fame of Jesus.

And said unto his servants, This is John the Baptist; he is risen from the dead; and therefore mighty works do shew forth themselves in him.

For Herod had laid hold on John, and bound him, and put him in prison for Herodias' sake, his brother Philip's wife."

Matthew 14:1-3

One of the key factors assisting one's understanding of everlasting life is better clarity of the role of the flesh. Yeshua questioned his students as to what would happen to them if something happened to him. He took this opportunity to explain to them the insignificant role of the flesh as compared to that of the spirit. If he taught that those who believed in him would never die, then certainly the servant is not greater than the master. He most definitely had to feel or believe that he himself would never die. He had to be alluding to the fact that to become discarnate would not mean that he was dead. This would have to imply that there are those who, through the power of God, have been or shall be made eternal beings. For those that believe in God, there seems to be a gift of God that sanctifies them even as they depart from the detection of the carnal eye. In the Hebrew language the word "life" is both plural and singular, indicating "lives" as well as "life." Therefore, the term "eternal life" could also be rendered as "eternal lives." Life thereby would be made eternal through cycles, the same as the cycles of a tree or the fruit thereof.

This gift's eternal provenance is obedience to the commandments and instructions of God. There is a relationship with God that allows man to pass into a realm of what is called perpetuity. It certainly stands to reason that Yeshua, Moses and the prophets would not be recognizable by their flesh if they were in the people's midst today. Yet it certainly is possible, and more than likely probable, that these messengers of God were bequeathed the power to stay alive, for believing and living, and denying and dying have been since Genesis, and will be until the end of Judgment Day. Daniel Ben Gabriel postulates:

> *"Jesus knew that 'in the regeneration' a name would be raised up unto him spiritually. I will address those instructions, first using the erroneous translation of most Bibles, then giving an explanation as to how I arrived at the conclusion which better relays in modern English the Hebrew thought that was conveyed (via the Greek language):*
>
> *And Jesus said unto them, 'Verily I say unto you that ye which have followed me, in the regeneration when the Son of man shall sit on the throne of his glory, ye also shall sit upon twelve thrones, judging the twelve tribes of Israel'.*
>
> *How is the parent the child and the child the parent in the temporal sense? GENES. Certainly genes are some aspect of all our beings. Since Jesus was not afforded a temporal genetic line, he had to rely on his faith in God's Law (of relativity) and his own spirituality. The Greek word for regeneration, a compound, was palin-genos; palin means spiritual cycle (through the idea of oscillatory repetition), and genos (from which the word genes derived) means rebirth. Thus in the correct Hebrew thought*

it should be in English:

And Jesus said unto them, 'This I say unto you that have followed me. Through my spiritual descendant, the Son of Man shall sit on the throne of his glory, and you shall sit upon twelve thrones judging the twelve tribes of Israel'.

Another saying of Jesus misinterpreted because of erroneous translations would be:

In my Father's house are many mansions, if it were not so, then I would have told you. I go to prepare a place for you.

The Greek word translated into English as house was Oikas. Oikas meaning estate or property, was idiomatically (commonly) used as family. Menos, loosely translated as mansions, means continuance (through the idea of offspring). Whatever noun in a sentence that menos complemented, gave its meaning to menos. Menos only strengthened the meaning. For example, first a house, then a menos. You know that menos is mansion, the next logical off-shoot of house. In light of the correct use of Greek as used in ancient days, below is presented the correct translation the Hebrew thought would have conveyed:

"In my Father's family there are means of continuing other than through your offspring, if it were not so then would I have told you? I shall depart, but ye shall share the same future prepared for me."

Here, in line with the above noted Mosaic Law, and in the Hebrew thought, Jesus inferred to his disciples that they too would have a 'spiritual rebirth' as opposed to rebirth through direct descendance, even though some of them surely had children. However, that direct line of descent would not be preserved."

The Alternative (A New Perspective on History, Jesus and the Law) by Daniel Ben Gabriel

After the fall of Adam and confusion of tongues, the merciful God of Creation gave the same pure, fundamental redemptive plan to chosen men around the world. These men passed these ideas of God to their respective nations. Each nation's interpretive application of these fundamentals was an amalgamation of the idea and each nation's respective cultural traits. The satanic objective has been/is in all of these nations to confuse the people through the creation of polemical opposition. In most contemporary countries, this has been done through the disguise of democracy.

The word of God warns us of the sordid state of man's affairs. Today "satan has confused, deceived the whole world," whereas God instructs us through the prophet Isaiah "seek ye the old paths wherein was the good life." In other words, halt your downward spiral called "progress" and turn back toward the Genesis under the guidance of ancient wisdom. Except that we move expediently, "there will be no flesh left alive on this planet." The great majority of the earth's inhabitants have been led into the pursuit of the mundane instead of the spiritual, the true essence of their being. What is spiritual? Spiritualism is the God-given ability to hear, discern and do truth. If it is true spiritualism, its origin is in a spirit that exists or a spirit that has been attained. Yeshua said "my sheep shall hear my voice," i.e. believe my words and do what I tell them. He also reminded us..."even the spirit of truth; whom this world cannot receive, because it sees Him not, neither knows Him." It is imperative that you take heed. The spirit to which I am referring is the "Spirit of Truth."

I emphasize this lest you forget that there are evil spirits also, vying for the souls of men. Negative spirits are actively struggling to maintain their (satan's) rule over you and the human family. These spirits control all evil nations. You are presently being held captive by them. Your problem is that you don't have the knowledge which would enable you to escape.

"And I saw three unclean spirits like frogs come out of the mouth of the dragon, and out of the mouth of the beast, and out of the mouth of the false prophet.

For they are the spirits of devils, working miracles, which go forth unto the kings of the earth and of the whole world, to gather them to the battle of that great day of God Almighty."

Revelations 16:13-14

"Then said he unto me, Fear not Daniel: for from the first day that thou didst set thine heart to understand, and to chasten thyself before thy God, thy words were heard, and I am come for thy words.

But the prince of the kingdom of Persia withstood me one and twenty days: but lo, Michael, one of the chief princes, came to help me; and I remained there with the kings of Persia."

"Then said he, Knowest thou wherefore I come unto thee? and now will I return to fight with the prince of Persia: and when I am gone forth, lo, the prince of Grecia shall come.

But I will shew thee that which is noted in the scripture of truth: and there is none that holdeth with me in these things, but Michael your prince."

Daniel 10:12-13, 20-21

John posited the existence of very powerful evil spirits performing some very convincing works before both ruler and layman. We must take special note that these great, miraculous achievements are used to deceive the inhabitants into making war against God. This war has already begun, for satan has created an insatiable appetite for greed, and initiated the unbridled pursuit of self-destruction. The people are poised to make war with all of us that have come to challenge their unholy lifestyles. Satan has thoroughly convinced them that we (God) are their enemy. Indeed the evil emissaries are of the world; they speak to the world and the world heareth them. We are of God. He that knows God hears us. He that is not of God does not hear us. We know the spirit of Truth and the spirit of error. Yeshua warns us of these spirits that have so assiduously mastered the art of lying, to the extent of being capable of deceiving the very elect. Evil now seems harmless; if not apprehended, it will cause the discontinuation of your lifespan on this planet. In retrospection, I hear you shouting: "Crucify him, Crucify him. We desire that Barabas be free!" Although the evil spirits prolong your suffering and misery, direct results of your depraved actions against those whom God has sent unto you, you still clamor for more evil.

We hear quite often the talk of spiritualism: "This is spiritual" or "I'm more or I'm less spiritual." What does this actually imply? In most cases it is merely a common figure of speech, uttered with little or no understanding. In addition to that, all spiritualism is not of God. Spiritualism from above implies that the individual has reached a plateau whereon he/she is an eternal spirit or in touch with, or in harmony with those that are eternal spirits.

"The wind bloweth where it willeth, and thou hearest the sound thereof, but canst not tell whence it cometh, and whither it goeth: so is every one that is born of the Spirit."

John 3:8

"But the hour cometh, and now is, when the true worshippers shall worship the Father in spirit and in truth: for the Father seeketh such to worship him.

God is a Spirit: and they that worship him must worship him in spirit and in truth."

John 4:23-24

"It is the spirit that quickeneth; the flesh profiteth nothing: the words that I speak unto you, they are spirit, and they are life."

John 6:63

"A good man sheweth favour, and lendeth: he will guide his affairs with discretion.

Surely he shall not be moved forever: the righteous shall be in everlasting remembrance."

Psalms 112:5-6

Spoken words are like the wind; they cannot be seen. They have no image or form. You hear the sound, but you cannot tell where it comes from or where it goes. Words are so alive until they penetrate your heart and mind, sometimes making you wise, and sometimes making you a fool; sometimes causing much joy, and too often, much pain. It is with words that you honor or deny. With a word, God came, and without that word, the Sons of God died. It certainly stands to reason that if the Sons of God died without the neshama (spirit), they

97

cannot meet the same fate if it is alive in them. Remember, death carries no positive connotations. To imply that someone is dead is to imply that they passed on without God (the *neshama*). Nevertheless, I am aware that I/you can't operate outside of the parameters of language. That is to say, I, too, was once hard pressed to express the whereabouts of the prophets without the initial use of the term dead. Therefore, the use of this term without an accompanying spiritual explanation would lead to misunderstanding and leave you hanging in space.

You must continue to call to mind that that which giveth life does not get buried in the graveyard. The flesh that is buried is not the determinant that the individual is dead. The body is composed of minerals. In fact, it's nothing but minerals and water, otherwise dirt. The body void of the spirit gradually decomposes (returns to the dirt). However, from that same dirt we grow the food which we eat. The question then remains: at what stage is man actually dead, before or after the decomposition of the body? The answer is simply before the decomposition, because the dirt or minerals are alive; otherwise, they could not produce life. The body, therefore is only dead without the living spirit of God. Subsequently, a resurrection in the graveyard would prove fruitless because that which giveth life would not/could not be there. Those that passed on in the flesh without the breath of life must experience eternal damnation which began the very first day they turned aside from the Eternal, blessed be He.

All men of God that become spirit are like the wind; they lose image, shape and form. In a search for body form, these men cannot be found; they can only be found and properly identified through spiritual discernment. The promise of the merciful God is that if you are sincerely in search of truth, you can hear truth. If you seek to know the spirit with all of your heart, soul and might, it shall be given unto you.

The prophet Isaiah spoke concerning the Messianic spirit. He elucidates (in the Hebrew text): "He has no description nor majesty, yet we shall see him. He has no form, yet we shall desire him." Isaiah also spoke of how carnal men have disfigured and disgraced him more than any man in their attempt to give this spirit tangible form. There

98

are those that we know that have been made eternal spirits. Yeshua knew he was not going to die, nor those that could hear and believe him. The inspired prophets are not dead; neither is David, Elijah or Enoch. Yeshua once asked his disciples "Whom do men say that I the Son of Man am?" And they said, "Some say thou art John the Baptist, some Elijah, and others Jeremiah or one of the prophets."

Except when considered in the sphere of the spiritual, this would be a question completely out of context. Carnally, what could the response have possibly been except whatever name he used to identify himself? Continuing on, he inquired "But whom say ye that I am?" (What is your response when questioned?) Peter's answer: "Thou art the Anointed Son of God." Yeshua's response: "Flesh and blood did not reveal this unto you, but the heavenly spirit of my Father." It is evident from the people's responses that they either expected these men to return or at least knew that they could. There were those that knew these men were alive with the power to come and go as eternal spirits. That means that in actuality, the expectations of what is now called erroneously the "second coming" is not/was not new. Many already expected certain figures to come again.

"Incline your ear, and come unto me. Hear, and your soul shall live; and I will make an everlasting covenant with you, even the sure mercies of David. Behold, I have given him for a witness to the people, a leader and commander to the people."

Isaiah 55:3-4

With those words the Throne of David was eternalized, symbolizing the seat of authority. It will not be one made with the hands of men, neither shall a king wearing a crown occupy it.

"For the children of Israel shall abide many days without a king, and without a prince, and without a sacrifice, and without an image, and without an ephod, and without teraphim:

Afterward shall the children of Israel return, and seek the Lord their God, and David their king; and shall fear the Lord and his goodness in the latter days."

Hosea 3:4-5

"And I will set up one shepherd over them, and he shall feed them, even my servant David; he shall feed them, and he shall be their shepherd.

And I the Lord will be their God, and my servant David a prince among them; I the Lord have spoken it.

And I will make with them a covenant of peace, and will cause the evil beasts to cease out of the land: and they shall dwell safely in the wilderness, and sleep in the woods."

Ezekiel 34:23-25

"Behold, I will send you Elijah the prophet before the coming of the great and dreadful day of the Lord:

And he shall turn the heart of the fathers to the children, and the heart of the children to their fathers, lest I come and smite the earth with a curse."

Malachi 4:5-6

As we peruse the words of Hosea, Ezekiel and Malachi, we discern that the notion of a second coming was not conceptualized solely for or during the time of Yeshua's ministry. The inspired prophets also forecast the second coming of David and Elijah. David explained that he would return in the likeness of God, quickened by an identifiable spirit. Elijah was to restore order to the family, and Yeshua called for a return to the original intent of the law. Through false art work and movies, the adversary of God has been very subtly trying to give form to these spirits to enhance deception and to a great extent, he has succeeded in making the eyes sharp and the ears dull.

As we have considered the fallacy of the Apostate Church's doctrine of the "second coming," let us continue with an examination of the familiar "calling on Jesus." Satan has again used deception to confuse the masses and the message concerning "calling" on spirits. I will do my utmost to make this dissertation comprehensible to all. Nevertheless, keep in mind that spiritual victories championed by the Holy One of Israel are won by means and upon principles that appear out of context in the view of human wisdom.

"THE GOOD SHIP JESUS"

"In 1562, 1564, and 1567, Sir John Hawkins carried cargoes of slaves from their native Africa to the West Indies and the Spanish Main. Several English noblemen including Queen Elizabeth had a financial interest in these voyages. The trade was a violation of Spanish law and ultimately Hawkins was attacked.

One of Sir Hawkins' ships, the "Jesus of Lubeck" sailed to the ports of Guinea and the West Indies in the years 1567 and 1568. The ship's name was changed and called "The Good Ship Jesus." The Christianized peoples of the Spanish Main associated the ship's name (Jesus of Lubeck) with Biblical history, and said that since Jesus was doing such good things for the poor, then Sir John Hawkins - in transporting African peoples from the African Continent to the New World - indeed was doing a good thing, because these peoples would become 'civilized' in the Americas."

**<u>Declaration of the Troublesome Voyage of Sir John Hawkins
to Guinea and the Indies</u>, Da Capo Press, Inc, 1973.**

To the great majority of the slaves this was their first hearing of the name Jesus. In the new lands the slavers exploited the enslavement of our people through the use of Jesus' name, trying to convince the slaves that since Jesus brought them to these new lands they should

101

consider themselves blessed. They were taught to remember that the "Good Lord (ship) Jesus" was in fact saving them from themselves. The slaves of the early years never accepted this, although many of them began to call on God to send Jesus back to get them. They were initially referring to the ships that had brought them into those cruel lands. Their minds were almost always on Jesus (the ships), wanting them (him) to come and take them home again. All of this has changed now as we witness the transformation of what was early on devised as a metaphorical misnomer to acceptable contemporary terminology. The truth is that the use of this name will not bring you into contact with nor activate the Holy Spirit on your behalf.

Calling upon spirits certainly is not new in African Edenic culture. Calling upon deceased ancestors is still very much a part of African spiritual expression - part of a faith that dates back thousands of years and has prevailed unto this day. But now after centuries of being exposed to Euro-centric apostate religion, they know not what they call upon. Their new traditions have made the word of God concerning holy spirits of none effect. Their new spiritualism is devoid of substance; it is all part of contemporary religious entertainment, an excellent imitation, yet not effective when you need the real thing.

If the ancients already believed in seeking assistance from spirits, then why and at what point in history did the religious myth begin? When was our spiritual power rendered ineffective? Is African Edenic spiritualism and Euro-centric spiritualism on the same plane? If so, were they in the days of our biblical predecessors? Has Euro-centric paganistic spiritualism supplanted genuine spiritualism in the midst of African Edenic people all over this planet? These are very pertinent questions. You had best consider well before answering. The ancient Hebrews calling upon an ancestor that they deemed to have power with God, and the apostate church's calling on Jesus are from two different worlds of spiritualism.

The laws given unto our fathers by Moses certainly delineated the need for an intercessor when one felt or knew he/she had fallen from the good graces of God. This individual would lose the right to come before the Throne of God on his own behalf. He would thus have to seek someone discarnate or incarnate to make intercession for him.

Moses was/is an intercessor. The priests, prophets, and certain kings and individuals were believed to have power with God and were trusted to speak on the sinners behalf.

No doubt everyone had faith in such a spirit or spirits. There is no denying that there were those who felt such a distinction was attributed to Yeshua of Nazareth. He certainly presented himself as an intercessor and those that believed him undoubtedly found many occasions to seek his assistance, asking that he make intercession on their behalf. Nevertheless you should open your mind to meditation and follow this Hebraic African Edenic spiritual custom as it is proliferated in pagan Greco-Roman society. Then you will have a better understanding of when and how this transformation took place. Not in your wildest imagination could you fathom that what arrived from the African Israelites and what was finally disseminated were one in spirit or substance. Has the power of our ancient spirituality been handed back to us from Rome, Canterbury, Germany, etc. on a silver platter unadulterated? Have they given us the keys to our spiritual power?

In your search for a better understanding of spirits there are two primary components that are essential. One is to believe in the Holy Spirit and the second is to believe in the power of the Holy Spirit. In the Holy Tongue the same word is used for both wind and spirit. It thus becomes evident that the Holy Spirit is like unto the wind. You don't know the wind by pointing it out as if it has an identity. You know the wind by what you feel and determine is a result of its presence. Possibly some of you recall that in earlier editions of the Bible the term "Holy Ghost" was used frequently. A ghost is the spirit of a supposedly deceased person which appears or otherwise makes its presence known to certain individuals. The only additional clarity needed at this time is that Holy Spirits are not people that have died but individuals that have been transformed, some of which have been given control of the active Power of God. They are also active in the service of those anointed by God. I am certain that when Yeshua prayed for those that were given him to be with him after his departure, he was asking that they be transformed into Holy Spirits that they may continue to behold His glory in the higher realms of spirituality. He

103

knew that man could be/was supposed to be an eternal being, with the power of incarnation as part of his God image and likeness/Divinity. I bear witness that you would be remiss to conclude that a/the discarnate Holy Spirit is in any way dead. Here I might add that it is not wrong to believe in and call upon the Holy Spirit of the biblical historical Yeshua. This does not negate the fact that there are other Holy Spirits also that can be called upon. Nevertheless, if they are not called upon, you must believe that they exist as living forces acting on behalf of the Holy One of Israel.

In his book <u>Before The Mayflower,</u> Lerone Bennett documented the often-denied historical fact: the slaves knew their God was the God that delivered the Israelites.

> *"The religion taught the slaves was a censored pablum which dwelt almost always on the duties of obedience. J. W. Fowler of Coahoma County, Mississippi, told his overseer that he had no objection to his slaves hearing the gospel if they heard it in its 'original purity and simplicity.' What did this mean? Ephesians 6:5, usually: 'Servants be obedient to them that are your masters...'*
>
> *Few slaves accepted this version of Christianity. Their God was the God who delivered the Israelites."*

<u>Before the Mayflower: A History of the Negro in America</u>
by Lerone Bennett, Jr., Johnson Publishing Co.

How and why is it that as late as the sixteenth century the Euro-centric name "Jesus" and contemporary Christianity had not found acceptance in Africa? Historically Africans, while they remained a free people, did not accept the European Jesus or the new religion connected with his name. Yet they knew in great detail of the Northeastern African Israelites, their prophets and anointed personages, including Yeshua. Nevertheless the slavemasters' version of events and the Holy Land sounded new and very strange. This Euro-centric version had to literally be forced upon our fathers.

> *"If the American white man fancies that he was the first to teach the Bible to his black slave, he is quite mistaken. A number of the African travelers have testified to African acquaintance with the Christian Bible. Jobson, for example, writes of the knowledge by Gambian natives in the early seventeenth century of Adam and Eve, whom they called 'Adam and*

Evahaha', Noah's flood, and Moses. . . Mungo Park, as affirmed by Marion L. Starkey, found that Fantooma, the Kaffir schoolmaster, had Arabic versions of the Pentateuch, the Psalms of David, and the Book of Isaiah. The unlettered Mandingoes entertained him with stories of Joseph and his brethren, Moses, David, and Solomon. They gave out the stories as part of their own folklore and were much surprised to learn that white men had heard them. If many slaves already knew a great deal of the Bible, the whole pattern of the origin and development of the backgrounds of the spiritual in America will have to be reconsidered.

The Africans were deeply and perpetually religious, using religion and religious song as a motive for being and expression along many lines. For the American whites religion was a Sunday or Wednesday night release from problems; as soon as the service was over, the church-goer reverted to his normal practice, which in many respects was diametrically opposed to his religious professions. "

Black Song: The Forge and the Flame
by John Lovell, Jr.,
Paragon House Publishers, New York, 1986

I bring to your attention the portion of the Messianic conspiracy that pertains to names. I am focusing on three languages: Hebrew, Greek and English, as they have played the dominant roles in Biblical translations. Approximately two thousand years ago, the Holy One of Israel ordained a messenger in the midst of His people, the Children of Israel. His name at birth was Yeshua Ben (the son of) Yoseph. After his ministry began, he was referred to by his followers as "The Messiah" (an anointed, consecrated person).

"The Euro-gentile Greek interpolators, while attempting to crush rebellion, always sought to prevent the rise of a Messiah in the midst of the Israelites. They inaugurated the process of 'name sacrilege'. They had been well-taught by their spiritual mentors that men of high, spiritual sensitivity should always pronounce the name of the anointed with profound accuracy. Their first test of 'name sacrilege' was initiated with Yeshua the Messiah. They transformed his name, thus successfully transforming his character (in the minds of the people) and amputated his message from its prophetic body. In my book, God the Black Man and Truth (Chapter 'The Making of a Slave or Soul Transformation'), I explain

in greater detail the consequences of being 'called out of your name.' By calling Yeshua Ben Yoseph 'Jesus Christ,' the Euro-gentiles successfully transformed the spirit of the man and his message to conform to their scheme. How was this accomplished? They gave him a Greek name and then created an image and personality which would be in agreement. Very few people are aware that in spelling and pronunciation, the name 'Jesus Christ' is totally Greek. The English derivatives are in harmony with the Greek, not the Hebrew syntax."

The Messiah and the End of This World
by Ben Ammi, Communicators Press

"And in all things that I have said unto you, be circumspect; and make no mention of the name of other gods, neither let it be heard out of thy mouth."

Exodus 23:13

At some point during the struggle between the Sons of Light (proponents of Godliness) and the sons of darkness (proponents of evil and injustice), satan (the prince of darkness) decided to take the bold step of transforming himself into an angel of light. In other words, he portrayed himself, not as the red-clad, forked-tail devil many would have you believe satan to be, but instead cloaked his evil ways and doctrine in a manner that would deceive you. Generally speaking, the most evil, destructive villains are usually the pillars in the neighborhood. Look at the priests in New Mexico reported on television's "60 Minutes" as molesters of innocent children. Well, in this same way, satan, in order to effectively deceive you, threw his pitchfork away and donned a clerical collar. Following his guidance, his ministers also transformed themselves into ministers of righteousness. Light is used synonymously in the Bible as the intellect of God - that which helps you to find your way. Therefore we can conclude that satan and his teachers are now wolves dressed in the lambs' clothing of religion. God promised us a light; but satanic spirits have now somehow manipulated their way into the high places as God's messengers. To the carnal eye the two opposites now appear synergetic as they both talk about God.

We have been taught by the prophets that there can be no righteous confluence between good and evil. The forces of evil had/have but one objective, that is/was to neutralize the effectiveness of truth, the Word of God, and to prevent active contact with the spirits that can help the Sons of Light defeat the sons of darkness. Here then is the scenario; satan is talking, teaching about God in some manner whereby you will not learn of the True God. He is articulating a worship of God that when applied will be the worship of him. (See "The True Worship of God", God the Black Man and Truth.) He has built structures called "Houses of God" which are in fact his unholy habitation. He now has the bedeviled masses calling on and activating spirits that assist him in maintaining control over the earth's inhabitants.

Let us not be deceived, little children. No Euro-centric religious doctrine will lead us to the desired and much-needed salvation. In whatever manner it may appear on the surface, harmless or calm, there is a strong, deadly undercurrent in religions that will sweep us away into the depths of hell and damnation. This has been shown and proven time and time again. For all the church-going, praying, talking in tongues, and unswerving allegiance shown to the church, religion has not diminished crime, unwed motherhood, war, or disease. What good has it been to you if society is not improved, your family relationship is not improved, or if at every turn, fear of something (government or the law) or someone (your neighbor's drug-dealing kid or the thugs your children attend school with) consumes your every waking moment?

Everything brought to us from Europe is divisive; it leaves us with a dual existence and purpose. His thousands of religions divide us; his unholy, unrestrained pursuit of material wealth divides us; his ungodly standards of manhood and womanhood divide us. Everything that satan has given us is the seed or fruit of dissension. Consequently we are weak before the strong and foolish before the wise. Yet, it stands to reason, if you could deduce the process by which you could be free and you were given the necessary teachings (keys) in his institutions of learning, then you would have applied your training to the attainment of freedom long ago. Instead, after years of study in his institutions and the subsequent application of these teachings to the struggle for liberation, Africans and African Americans continuously fall short of the mark. A world that desires to keep us powerless and enslaved cannot afford to give us, the oppressed, the teachings that will free us, nor a God that will save us. A tyrant that desires to keep you weak, cannot give you a history which will make you strong.

"Calling on spirits" is in the same category as the "second coming." It is not new; it was always referred to and employed by our fathers. It was a power and phenomenon greatly feared by the slave masters when we were brought to the Americas. They gave it the misnomer "Black Magic," made its practice illegal and attempted to annihilate or denigrate all that used it or believed in its powers. After an extensive campaign of persecution most of those who understood calling on spirits were driven underground, ostracized and discredited because of the multiplicity of negative connotations attached to the practice. Soon thereafter there was to come forth the cunning missionaries teaching about new spirits and demanding that they be called upon. Thus began the transformation from true spiritualism to religious commercialism, seances, familiar spirits, etc., which would cause all the former emphasis to be lost or forgotten.

> *"Then he answered and spoke unto me, saying, this is the word of the Lord unto Zerubbabel, saying, not by might, nor by power, but by my spirit, saith the Lord of Hosts."*
>
> **Zechariah 4:6**

> *"Thy nakedness shall be uncovered, yea, thy name shall be seen; I will take vengeance, and I will not meet thee as a man."*
>
> **Isaiah 47:3**

> *"Surely the Lord God will do nothing, but he revealeth his secret unto his servants, the prophets."*
>
> **Amos 3:7**

From the aforementioned scriptural references we may safely conclude that we are not to visualize God as being physically active in the affairs of men. He maintains all contact and carries out all actions by way of an army of Holy Spirits. (Among the compound names used to identify the Creator is the "Lord of Hosts" [or "Armies"].) Many of these Holy Spirits are saints that were formerly alive and active in God's service on this earthly plane. These Holy Spirits can be activated according to the Will of God by men in God's service through prayer, meditation, abstention and the need to carry out His instructions.

Our people were always in contact with, or calling upon these spirits to assist them as seasons required. Therefore, we can imagine without much effort that in the course of a normal day full of blessings and problems, there would be those giving thanks for the assistance received from the Holy Spirit, and others crying out for mercy and help. Remember, everything that would give strength had to be taken away. You've been subtly deceived into commiting sacrilege toward the God that can save you. When satan disguised himself as an angel of light it was also to gain access to the hidden intellect concerning your demise and subsequent rise. He would soon thereafter activate his master plan to keep you in captivity. My people now having lost all former power are victims to all of the weaker spirits and are now helplessly consumed all the day long. They have abided many days without the true God, teaching priests and the Law of God. Thus, because of a lack of knowledge they have no strength to fight back.

We need only to open our eyes to see that the evil spirits have prevailed against the Sons of Light until these the days of the Kingdom of God. The Saints of the Most High have come alive and shall break in pieces all of these evil kingdoms (unholy spirits) and shall stand forever. Nevertheless the former standard bearers of God have been seduced into maintaining a lifestyle which continuously shows contempt for the God of Creation and His Holy Spirits.

"As it is written in the law of Moses, all this evil is come upon us: Yet made we not our prayer before the Lord our God, that we might turn from our iniquities, and understand his truth."

Daniel 9:13

There are holy spirits that are always moving to and fro on and around the earth. These angelic beings are in control of certain elements and attributes which are to be used to assist the forces of righteousness. Joshua was guided by an unseen, always present Holy Spirit that revealed himself prior to the fall of Jericho. Saul knew that he was naked without the guidance of God through a prophet or a dream. Thus he knew that Samuel was still an active spirit although he could no longer activate him. He subsequently sought out a sorcerer with a familiar spirit to revive the spirit of Samuel. Daniel prayed and made sincere supplications before God and he was sent the angel Gabriel which had the power to give him a mind by which to understand.

This is the same angel which came in 1966 to me to give me the mind to understand the prophecies connected with the exodus of the African Hebrews and establishing of the Kingdom of God (See "Introduction" God the Black Man and Truth, and The Impregnable People by Prince Gavriel HaGadol). Yeshua went up into the mountain and called out in prayer for guidance and he was sent Moses and Elijah to talk with him concerning things to come. When is the last time you called on Moses, Elijah, Gabriel, Michael, Rifael, David, Samuel or any of the other Holy Spirits? How did Daniel pray to be heard by God? How did the prophets, David, Yeshua and Moses pray? Look around you and let your condition discern the spirit that is active in your midst. How did we that once sat so high come down so low, accepting a sacrosanct religion that has obviously taken us so far away from God the Father and Truth? Behold, the Holy Spirit of the Lord God is upon me, because the Lord has anointed me to preach good tidings unto the meek; He hath sent me to bind up the brokenhearted, to proclaim liberty to the captives, and the opening of the prisons to them that are bound.

"Then said I, O my lord, what are these? And the angel that talked with me said unto me, I will shew thee what these be.

And the man that stood among the myrtle trees answered and said, These are they whom the Lord hath sent to walk to and fro through the earth.

And they answered the angel of the Lord that stood among the myrtle trees, and said, We have walked to and fro through the earth, and behold, all the earth sitteth still, and is at rest."

Zechariah 1:9-11

"And after six days Jesus taketh Peter, James, and John his brother, and bringeth them up into an high mountain apart,

And was transfigured before them: and his face did shine as the sun, and his raiment was white as the light.

And, behold, there appeared unto them Moses and Elijah talking with him."

Matthew 17:1-3

"...Who maketh his angels spirits; his ministers a flaming fire."

Psalms 104:4

"And it came to pass, when I, even I Daniel, had seen the vision, and sought for the meaning, then behold, there stood before me as the appearance of a man.

And I heard a man's voice between the banks of Ulai, which called, and said, Gabriel, make this man to understand the vision."

Daniel 8:15-16

What are my predictions concerning the lifespan of true believers? I can't say accurately at this time, but time and hope will increase as you continue your journey believing these things I've shared with you. Nevertheless, joyfully, I will now increase your Holy expectations by saying inevitably it will be longer than Methusalah's 969 years. Why? Because even that lengthy lifespan was achieved after the fall of man. In addition to that, we joyfully speculate that where there is no cause, there is no effect.

Men have had the choice of being servants of God or satan since the fall of Genesis. It was at that time that God allowed the force of evil, (called satan, the devil, and Lucifer, the Father of a lie) to

111

challenge truth. Man, after his fall, would no longer find himself automatically in the service of God. He would have to make the right choice; he would have to master truth, or be ruled by deception. The lie would put him in opposition to God. This disgrace would weaken his power over err (satan) and death. Because of his fall in Eden, things that were once his perpetual possessions as gifts of life from God, were now attainable only through an overcoming of the forces of evil. As man inexorably spiralled downward in his self-deception, the need for saviors, deliverers or those anointed, increased, and with it the need for the written word. Nevertheless, truth has always existed, but men turned away from truth to follow a lie. Man has been imprisoned by falsehood, and only the truth can set him free.

Although it is impossible for a lie to completely eradicate or defeat truth, this nevertheless is the objective of the forces of evil. This war is to be waged between the Sons of Light and the sons of darkness until the time of the end. At the time of the end, the awakened sons of God, under the sovereignty of the Most High and armed with truth, will decimate the sons of darkness that were fashioned out of error.

Yeshua said that those of truth can hear truth; his sheep could hear his voice, and would not follow a stranger or a strange doctrine that would alienate them from God. You no doubt, have had the occasion to say "I hear myself in him" or "I see myself in him." If you, in your very low existence, can see and hear yourself in someone, are there those in higher realms that can not only see themselves, but can see others?

We have been taught that the pure in heart shall see God. Yet we know that the Omnipotent God has no flesh or similitude; even the Heaven of heavens cannot contain Him. Notwithstanding, the pure in heart will see God. Certainly if you can fathom seeing God, it should be a very small thing to see David and/or Elijah. You are admonished to seek the righteousness of the Kingdom and all other things would be added unto you. It is through your obedience to the Kingdom of God that you receive eyes to see and ears to hear. For there are those that have haughty eyes and see not; arrogant ears and hear not. These must bend down their backs to continued oppression. They love darkness more than light. They have fallen in love with and married a lover with no heart of flesh. Whatever way or manner, there is a realm wherein man shall see God. Flesh and blood will not be the determinants for it is by the spirit (word of God) that he shall reveal himself. Therefore you must first hear before you can see and, moreover, understand what you are looking at. Other than that, your very destruction will stand before you, and you won't recognize it. You will neither recognize friend or foe of God and humanity. You won't see the destructive elements nor force of salvation.

When you can't hear the truth, or see evil, then your ears are dull and your eyes are blurred. The masses today have been seduced into pursuing the lower realms of modern science and technology instead of the ancient, everlasting upper domains of God's creativity. You look out into this morbid world and you define it as progressive. You can't imagine a mentality or intellect far beyond what is seen today. You are afraid to seriously consider that you exist in the sphere of an obdurate dominion that poisons its own food; pollutes its own water and air; sells poisons to friends and relatives knowingly; does not know how to have fun without destructive alcohol and cocaine; does not know how to share the basic needs of man; destroys food to support prices while others starve. Destruction is portrayed as fun (pinball and other war games); children are sold toy weapons that teach them elementary killing. These things and conditions could only exist because of a low level of intellectual development.

Long ago when the quest for God ceased, so did human development. When we look back and critically examine almost every facet of today's modern society, we readily and plainly see how far off we have gotten in the quest for God. Common sense has been replaced by uncommon nonsense and we have been given a concept of God which has not made us godly. Slave-oriented Christianity and its institutions have made us anything but "Christ-like" in our attitudes and actions. They have not strengthened our families, increased our brotherly love or inspired our honesty. Indeed, what we have been given has destroyed and undermined our sense of what is ethical, moral and "naturally" right.

Do we not surely need to go back to the very beginning? Search it out again? Seek the keys to true righteousness? If we no longer have righteous lifestyles and true culture, then we are set in a continuous cycle which excludes the instituting of love, truth, justice, mercy, equity and peace amongst men. All that can thus be left is the halting of human development and the eternal damnation of the race of man on earth. The process of human development is tied fast to the quest for God. When one ceases, the other must halt. We have come full cycle to the point where - if we are to go any further - we must begin again. For, due to the spiritual darkness of today, it is as it was in the beginning, "...the earth is without form and void...."

The process of human development is another phase of the quest for God. It is the progression of man's upward evolution toward his higher (true God) spiritual nature. Death was merely the chosen word to express the opposite of life. Man's existence, alienated from God, is called death. It could have been any word. It bears no mysterious connotations. Likewise, the suitable name for death's environment - "hell" - carries with it a thorough explanation of all the things that would befall the dead. The conclusion of that satanic dominion of darkness leaves man no longer in remembrance.

Once an individual separates himself from God, another existence comes into focus, filled with things befitting the dead. The master of this environment is like a salesman whose livelihood depends upon selling his product. He has to convince all potential buyers that his product is far superior to all others - no matter how inferior it really is. He has to develop a positive sales pitch, or his existence (income) will perish. Likewise, with satan, the arch enemy and competitor of God, his leadership, his domain, his products and followers, must be sold, given status, and made to appear as things desired.

Salesmen must be well trained, thus satan educates you to be his sales representatives. Every day and every way you sell an evil, worthless product. You rationalize evil behaviour in a variety of ways: smokers shun the Surgeon General's warning, saying "you gotta die some time;" you'll buy anything advertised on the T.V., totally unconcerned as to whether it's filled with chemicals that will destroy your health or damage the environment; and worst of all, you justify all your evil ways by going to church 3 out of 4 Sundays, believing by doing so, you can pray for forgiveness and all will be okay.

Besides, "you gotta die some time," so why not live life to the fullest? You first convince yourself, then your unsuspecting generations that hell is the best thing going. Certainly you must admit that a well-trained, educated salesman can sell an unaware person just about anything. Then in most cases, after you are told, or even you yourself realize that you have been a sucker, your pride won't let you confess that you made a bad deal. Most individuals never admit they were tricked. Sad, but it's true!

"Let no man deceive you by any means: for that day shall not come, except there come a falling away first, and that man of sin be revealed, the son of perdition;

Who opposeth and exalteth himself above all that is called God, or that is worshipped; so that he as God sitteth in the temple of God, shewing himself that he is God."

II Thessalonians 2:3-4

"The Lord is my light and my salvation; whom shall I fear? the Lord is the strength of my life; of whom shall I be afraid?"

Psalms 27:1

The end was preceded by a falling away from morality, signifying that the "son of perdition" must truly exist. The son of perdition is satan and satanic systems of government. The simultaneous existence of the Kingdom of God was a prerequisite to the season of the transition from the dominion of satan unto the dominion of God. It has presaged the last days of the dominion of satanic principles over God's creations. During this period of time, certain celestial and terrestrial events will take place to enhance the downfall of satan and the rise of Godliness, and thus God. During this epic struggle, a great light will come with the opening of the book (God mind), thus shining truth upon the obscurity caused by satan, whereby his evil systems and way of life (death) shall be judged and rejected. We are now in "Judgment Day" as we watch the daily revelations pouring from the different audio-visual networks and government agencies concerning the evil satan has wrought against the people and the creations of God.

When David, Yeshua and other Sons of God said that "I am the

115

light," they were using the term light in contrast or opposition to darkness, meaning that the intellect of God emanated from them. This was in contrast to the darkness - or intellect of satan, God's adversary - emanating from those of this world. This light is also synonymous with the presence of God, for light was seen by our Fathers as a thing or person. "I am the light" only means that "light (God and Godly intellect) emanates from me." This bright vision allows men of Godly realms to see, through God's wisdom, things not seen by the carnal eye. It was in this manner that Yeshua saw Elijah in the body of a man called John the Baptist. The common people also knew that Elijah was to come, but they being carnal as the nations are today, were looking for his flesh to identify his spirit, instead of his spirit to identify his flesh. Thus, instead of looking for a return of Yeshua, people should be listening for a return of Yeshua.

The truth about these things is being revealed now because the Kingdom of God has come. The call now is for repentance, to halt your support and praise for these evil milieus. Your salvation means that you must come out of this world and declare your allegiance unto God's Kingdom, and give your support to the building of a truly new world order. We cannot/shall not see injustices as normal. We cannot/should not accept the present evil societies and systems as the routine conducting of business for humanity; something innocuous that we should not change. Rather we should fear their continued existence, thus enhancing change for the sake of the future. New ideas of another realm of spiritual creativity should go forth at this time in history. We should not be afraid of heavenly ideas. As a matter of fact, we should long for them and rejoice at their coming. After all, it was the proliferation of new Euro-centric ideas that reduced humanity and our planet earth to its present state of ruin and chaos.

THE SEEDS OF EVIL -
THE GRACE OF TRUTH

As we study and attentively listen to the words of God spoken in Genesis concerning life and death, the message is clear. To attain everlasting life was not an objective or a possible plateau which one could reach. Everlasting life was the eternal gift of God unto His creations - man and nature. We know this to be a truth since man was told that he would die only if he ate of the tree of good and evil. This might appear to be an excessive sentence for the crime, until we see and realize what the proliferation of evil has done. The dominion of the spirit of err has been devastating.

Why is it that such a definite statement was made concerning good and evil trees? A tree becomes a tree through the seed of the fruit it bears. The fruit is grown according to the seed planted in the soil. Just as the seed of a tree maintains a continuous hereditary line, the seeds of evil continue to yield similar fruit. The ongoing process never changes. As long as this evil tree is allowed to grow, it will only yield adulterated fruit. This is the reason that God has promised "the seed of evildoers shall be cut off." This fruit (thoughts, ideologies, philosophies and religion), will always be diametrically opposed to God and truth. The old seed has to die and a new seed has to be

117

planted, causing new life to spring forth with an entirely different outlook and direction, becoming a tree of life, bearing fruit of itself, that yields the works (worship) of God, obedience to His plan and can sustain eternal life. Evil does not allow anyone - not one soul - to enjoy total life or the creations of God.

Once man ate of the forbidden doctrine, he was removed from the Edenic garden of paradise. Why? Adam had been explicitly instructed not to eat of this tree. Thus after disobeying the Creator, his maker, the sentence in its entirety had to be served. Man was driven from the Garden of Eden or from his natural habitation with God to the abnormal; from being a vessel under the dominion of God's love to become a vessel under the dominion of satan's hate, enmity, greed, lust, sickness and death. Thus it is clear that whatever Adam had become after eating the forbidden fruit, made him an object of scorn unacceptable unto God, his maker. This tragic event is also the inception of man's need for the process of redemption. Redemption is the primary need of a ruined race. To redeem is to free from what distresses or harms. To extricate from or help to overcome something detrimental; to free from captivity by payment or ransom. Who or what holds my people in captivity? "His own iniquities shall take the wicked himself, and he shall be held with the cords of his sins." (Proverbs 5:22) Their spiritual transformation brought them into conflict with God and has caused their demise. What is the payment required? Someone has to tell them the truth and suffer the consequences.

"And ye shall know the truth, and the truth shall make you free."

John 8:32

The great majority of the social crises facing our people today are but symptoms of an underlying spiritual conflict. Our people's way of life (death) perpetuates their opposition to God. This obvious aversion to God causes their physical degeneracy, a by-product of spiritual degeneracy. Spiritual degeneracy is the direct result of a people being taught wrong. (In the beginning it was the Word, or correct teachings). The problems of our people can be traced to our leaders; we are faced with a crisis in leadership!

"Whatever structure a leader is functioning under, he or she functions within the parameters of that structure. The only way to maintain themselves and progress within that structure is to seek the interests of that structure or system. This is true whether in politics, music, economics, or social structures - there are laws that govern the system. Black leadership is trapped in the system."

Dr. Leonard Owens , "Crisis in Leadership,"
Jerusalem Viewpoint, Winter 1991

Where are the redeemers who are willing to pay the price required? Who is willing to suffer embarrassment of his own past in order to bring forth solutions for both the present and the future? Who will tell them they do not worship the true God? Who will tell them that they are trapped in hell, not going to heaven, dying instead of living, hating instead of loving, destroying instead of building, and have never - neither will they ever - taste of freedom in this present world system? Who are they that are willing to pay the price and suffer the consequences thereof? Understandably, the harvest is great and the laborers are few. I call Heaven and Earth as my witnesses: if there was another way I would have told you so. It is time to be valiant for the truth.

During this redemptive process, I must teach you about the true God-proper worship and communion, because we have truly forgotten how to pray. This truth will cause renewed movement and Holy visibility back unto God and will cause you to pass through many hostile scenes (mental) enroute to a/the promised inheritance. All of those who are seeking, must understand that anointed leadership is the focal point of a redemptive struggle. The people are not/shall never be left without a form of leadership. Let us not be naive, the destruction of the people also depends upon detrimental leadership. The polemical phalanx of the sons of darkness is the most evident provenance of contemporary problems and/or obstacles placed before the Sons of Light. The sons of darkness have been positioned as the front line confrontational forces to prevent the advancement of truth. Also there are designated, masterminded criteria given to all those ordained by the devil to slander and denounce the message of those sent by God.

When Noah was preaching the imminent end of the then existing

119

social system, there were other very astute leaders explaining, no doubt very articulately, why it could not happen. There was leadership before Moses' arrival in Egypt with his message. Also there was another class of leaders before and after Yeshua's death. The point of contention was that they were not anointed by God. So it is today. Subsequently, today's leaders can only lead you within the parameters allowed by the system. They cannot lead the necessary redemptive struggle. God anoints His redeemers and dispatches them to place the choice before the people: do you want to be a functionary in the system and receive a transitory fascination, or the redemption of your souls and a new life in a new world?

"For what is a man advantaged, if he gain the whole world, and lose himself, or be cast away?"

Luke 9:25

Since the fall of man into oblivion, redeemers have been necessary. Saviours have labored diligently to make their message understood, their objective being to make the people acceptable again unto God. Satan, the adversary of God, strives to steer them away from change or rebirth. His message is devious. He states that under the law it is utterly impossible to please or be acceptable unto God. His constant theme is that one day a God full of grace and mercy will overlook your need for spiritual discipline, and accept you as you are: a little devil that loves and sustains evil. He contends that regardless of whatever efforts you make to do right, you'll only fall short, so don't overdo this thing about righteousness.

God drove man from the garden for a testimony unto Him and the coming generations. Beware, lest we be remiss and believe that a deviant behavior would/could find acceptance with God. Be cautious of possessing a spirit of extrapolation, because in the final analysis, we must conclude that the Most High has a standard that must be met. Whether man attains this standard does not alter the fact that it exists, that is the Edenic truth. Man only deceives himself if he thinks that he has an option ("freedom of choice") regarding God's standard or code of ethics. This frame of thought causes him to be double-minded, and vacillate between good and evil. But the Almighty is expressedly at variance with such a disposition. In the corporeal sense, everlasting life was put beyond our reach; our access to it was blocked. Adam chose to eat of the forbidden fruit, therefore, we are in the abyss under the dominion of satan until we sincerely petition God from the depths of our soul. After escaping this dreadful experience, we will never want an option or "freedom of choice" again. God knows that's the truth! When this conflagration is extinguished, we will be perfectly content with a "one track mind," one that knows only God and goodness, that is.

From the time of Noah, Moses, Yeshua and even to this day, the redemptive message has been rejected by the masses. After each rejection, the plight of the people worsens. This process of rejecting saviors has a time limit. Afterwards, if necessary, God will take a minute few and use them to build a new world order. This epoch is known as the end of the season of persuasion. Yeshua stated that messengers would be sent to redeem the people, but they would be/have been rejected, consequently the people would forfeit those opportunities for redemption. Thus he made the conditions of acceptance clear: you shall acknowledge God's anointed and plan, or you will never receive salvation.

"O Jerusalem, Jerusalem, thou that killest the prophets, and stonest them which are sent unto thee, how often would I have gathered thy children together, even as a hen gathereth her chicks under her wings, and ye would not!

Behold, your house is left unto you desolate.

For I say unto you, Ye shall not see me henceforth, till ye shall say Blessed is he that cometh in the name of the Lord."

Matthew 23:37-39

Each savior brought an identical message. "Rebirth" is the prerequisite if you desire to be reunited with God. To accept change is to acknowledge the guilt of past years and past deeds. Man finds it difficult to accept guilt; his obstinacy impels him to try to hide it and he hardens his heart. Yeshua told the scholar Nicodemus "You must be born again" to inherit the Kingdom. Nicodemus was not cognizant

121

that he was unacceptable unto God. He was a man full of religious commitment and biblical knowledge, well versed in religious dogma and rituals. It had to be a painful moment indeed to come to the realization that he was imperfect. The truth is, his religious dogma transformed him, diverting him from following the laws of God to following the traditions of paganistic men.

One of the major areas of Euro-centric/Euro-gentile religious deception is to misinterpret the meaning of the biblical terms of "grace" and "mercy," thereby leaving the layman vulnerable to the machinations of the devil.

"Even so then at this present time also there is a remnant according to the election of grace.

And if by grace, then is it no more of works: otherwise grace is no more grace. But if it be of works, then is it no more grace: otherwise work is no more work."

Romans 11:5-6

In a contemporary or religious sense, these verses are interpreted to mean that your lawful works for God lose their status and stature once you've been exposed to grace. This interpretation is inaccurate and misleading, conveying a false message to the recipient of God's grace.

Grace finds you in darkness, but it does not leave you there. When truth finds you wallowing in sin, it finds you by the grace of God. You have done nothing to deserve its presence. It did not find you by your works. It is proportionately true that every man judged by his works would have a blemish. But every mistake is not sin; mistakes not corrected become the product of an unruly spirit which transforms them into sin. However, the author of Romans, editor or interpolator has fallaciously distorted the original point about grace clarified by the Prophet Ezekiel. Furthermore, all New Testament writings or truths must be based upon the laws, prophecies and prophets of God.

In some instances, the New Testament writers and interpolators were simply endeavoring to explain those concepts within the context of a comprehensible salvation. Nevertheless, if there are writings that cannot be verified in the law or authenticated by the prophecies, it is prudent to forsake them. If the words conflict with or appear to contradict the words of the Prophets, seek clarification and explanation. If that is not possible, then hold fast to the words of the inspired prophets of God.

"Surely the Lord God will do nothing, but he revealeth his secret unto his servants, the prophets."

Amos 3:7

"Bind up the testimony, seal the law among my disciples.

And I will wait upon the Lord that hideth his face from the House of Jacob, and I will look for him.

Behold, I and the children whom the Lord hath given me are for signs and for wonders in Israel from the Lord of hosts, which dwelleth in Mount Zion.

And when they shall say unto you, Seek unto them that have familiar spirits, and unto wizards that peep, and mutter: should not a people seek unto their God? For the living to the dead?

To the law and to the testimony: if they speak not according to this word, it is because there is no light in them."

Isaiah 8:16-20

We find the term "grace" throughout the Epistles (a series of letters written to different individuals and congregations some attributed to the Apostles and Paul.) The reigning contemporary understanding of "grace" and other terminology nullifies the restoration of the true worship of God, and the critical need for new direction. Let me say at this point that it goes beyond the purpose of my writings, to examine every statement made by Paul. Through time and translations, much of the original texts and meanings have been certainly lost. Nonetheless, thanks be unto God the Most High and Holy One of Israel, unto whom all praises are due, I shall endeavor to enlighten you by decoding and clarifying within the framework of His comprehensible, affirmed truth. I am moved by the authority and spirit of God that is bequeathed unto me at this very critical juncture in our history and time.

To be graceful is to be thoughtful and considerate, not foolish. In Ezekiel we find grace personified. The Omnipotent God shows great kindness by giving you clemency, exempting you from judgment, for your past works; giving you the un-earned privilege to enjoy everlasting life. God has put your pardon papers in your hands, but they are conditional. Now you must maintain your allegiance unto Him. After receiving all of the blessings of life under God, not by works but by grace, what do you feel that God should require of you? This touches upon something known in the legal system as "parole."

An individual receives sentencing of, let us say, ten years, and after three years he is paroled for the remaining seven. During this seven years, he must abide by the condition of his parole board or officer. He must do what is lawful and right. Three years pass and the parolee is calling and reporting, doing what is required of him. But behold! After the three years, he violates his parole. Thus he is brought before the magistrate where he pleads: "Give me credit for the three years that I called and did what was required of me." Because he failed the seven year parole test, his previous three years of good conduct are rendered null and void. As a result, he has the full seven years staring him in the face. His good works are not taken into consideration: he will be judged by his criminal record, past and present.

If you can accept the justice meted out by the statutes of man, how much more in the statutes of God? If this is not the message of grace which Paul sought to convey, then Paul and those following him have a problem. An individual's works may not earn him grace, but only change for the better (as determined by works) will maintain it.

"The soul that sinneth, it shall die. The son shall not bear the iniquity of the father, neither shall the father bear the iniquity of the son; the righteousness of the righteous shall be upon him.

But if the wicked will turn from all his sins that he hath committed, and keep all my statutes, and do that which is lawful and right, he shall surely live; he shall not die.

All his transgressions that he hath committed, they shall not be mentioned unto him; in his righteousness that he hath done he shall live.

Have I any pleasure at all that the wicked should die? saith the Lord God; and not that he should return from his ways, and live?

But when the righteous turneth away from his righteousness, and committeth iniquity, and doeth according to all the abominations that the wicked man doeth, shall he live? All his righteousness that he hath done shall not be mentioned; in his trespass that he hath trespassed, and in his sin that he hath sinned, in them shall he die.

Yet ye say, The way of the Lord is not equal. Hear now, O house of Israel, Is not my way equal? Are not your ways unequal?

When a righteous man turneth away from his righteousness, and committeth iniquity, and dieth in them, for his iniquity that he hath done shall he die.

Again, when the wicked man turneth away from his wickedness that he hath committed, and doeth that which is lawful and right, he shall save his soul alive.

Because he considereth, and turneth away from all his transgressions that he hath committed, he shall surely live; he shall not die."

Ezekiel 18:20-28

This definition of grace is not attributed to, nor did it originate during, the New Testament apostolic period. The negative effects of deception are awesome. Mercy, grace, prayer and an intercessor are required to redeem your lost soul. For the Sons of Light wrestle not against flesh and blood, but against principalities and well-established religious beliefs; against powers; against the rulers of the darkness of this world; against spiritual wickedness in high places. The proletariat of the land has put on the whole armor of satan, and on his behalf strives diligently to prevent the slightest penetration of truth.

The summarization of the New World definition of "grace" is: an act or instance of kindness, clemency, or mercy; unmerited Divine assistance given man for his regeneration or sanctification. One may ascertain that grace is not/cannot be classified as a way of life. Allow me to give another brief example of grace, again, using a hypothetical situation for the sake of clarity.

Suppose that you are reading my book or attending my class for the first time. I've put hours, maybe even days into the preparation of my subject matter. Thereafter, the date, time and place are publicized. Sometimes my assistants have had to face difficult, and even hazardous conditions to knock on your door to inform you concerning the class to be held. Finally, I deliver my message and you are moved to respond positively and from that day henceforth you are a faithful soldier in the army of God. The day on which you heard my message will always be remembered as your salvation day. My question is thus: did your works save you or were you saved by the grace of God?

The sinner that persistently sits in the audience receives an abundance of unmerited Divine assistance. ALL of us were saved by the grace of God. God's mercy influenced the presence of the sinner in the class, not the works of the sinner. We all, through similar experiences, were brought to the light. Actually, who can boast that his works saved him? Furthermore, little children, it marks a new beginning if you understand that this kindness was for your regeneration. Grace brought you inside. Now you must behave like you want to stay inside. If you are to convince me that you know better, then you must do better (works). The epistle of Jude gives insight into the "grace" of the apostate teachers:

> *"Beloved, when I gave all diligence to write unto you of the common salvation, it was needful for me to write unto you, and exhort you that ye should earnestly contend for the faith which was once delivered unto the saints.*
>
> *For there are certain men crept in unawares, who were before of old ordained to this condemnation, ungodly men, turning the grace of our God into lasciviousness..."*
>
> **Jude 1:3-4**

Once you have sincerely declared your allegiance unto God - with all your heart, soul and might - God then promises to exonerate you of all of your past offenses against Him, and none of your former sins are to be remembered. He will be gracious not to make your past a stumbling block unto you. Nonetheless, from the day that you receive clemency, your every act and deed will be monitored by the Omnipresent spirit of God. And if you revert back to your old sinful ways, then none of your righteousness is significant. And you will be judged as one who turns aside (breaks his allegiance with God). Hear now the proverb of the builder.

It is like a man that builds a temple unto God today, then tomorrow he burns it to the ground. When he is brought before the throne of God unto judgment, he asks for consideration by stating "But yesterday I built a house of worship unto you. Consider my good in building the edifice when you judge me for burning it down." That would make it complex, to say the least. There you are, trying to determine which half is the most significant: the half of him that belongs to God or the half of him that belongs to satan. I can hear your decision and reasoning: set the prisoner free, for he has some good in him. Today he murders a citizen; tomorrow he pulls one out of the quicksand. He only kills every other day. That kind of society is well and good to all of those pulled out of the quicksand. They will no doubt argue on his behalf, but it is surely hell for those who were killed. As for myself, I do not want to live under those judges, dwell in their society nor partake of their world. I already know your next question is "why?" Because in your world I only have half a chance to live! He that has ears to hear, let him hear!

Thus God has taught us you cannot judge good and evil! You judge one or the other. There will be those saying my ways are not equal. But truthfully, it is a man's iniquities that kill him. I can only bring it to bear on one's conscious. The earth cannot be controlled by good and evil; it has to be one or the other. Those standing for God cannot allow the perpetual reign of wickedness. The good and evil nature is totally, biblically and truthfully, satanic. You, the masses, have been deceived by the satanic spirit of err and those controlled and motivated by it. With the power to define in the hands of God's/your enemy, he has interpreted everything to and about the captive in order to maintain his captivity. His objective is/was/always will be to prevent you from making the necessary change which would bring you back into the fold of God. Satan exists on evil; this is his nourishment. He has to have it. We can only destroy him if we eradicate evil from this earth.

"And I will put enmity between thee and the woman, and between thy seed and her seed; it shall bruise thy head, and thou shalt bruise his heel."

Genesis 3:15

Brethren, I beseech you to understand. There is perpetual enmity between the two seeds. They cannot co-exist. Co-existence would mean I would have to find pleasure in evil. But evil is injurious to me (bruises my heel), and right is dangerous to evil (bruises his head). When I see the wicked manufacturing and selling cigarettes, even to his own, I am troubled. By my nature I want him to cease. And when evil discerns that I don't smoke or condone the manufacturing of cigarettes, he is injured. By his evil nature, he desires that I partake in his evil machinations.

The God of love and righteousness obviously could not allow such a situation to prevail. We desire for all men to regain their immortality. If not, we would not proliferate these truths and make them available unto all men. As sons and daughters of God, we get no pleasure in watching the wicked die. It is not enjoyment for us to watch a cancer patient suffer. We are not entertained by watching the afflicted masses being tormented. The God within us is in great distress watching the scenes of death and destruction on the other side. Thus, since these things give us no pleasure but instead are a source of pain, it stands to reason, that in God's New World order, there will be no perpetuation of evil. The total eradication of the satanic mind and works is our platform.

THE TRUTH ABOUT DEATH

Life, and its enemy death, have always been shrouded with mystery, so much so that it would seem we were not supposed to understand them. Yet, not understanding them would not allow us to contribute to life's existence, or prevent death's occurrence, leaving man neutralized; man would conclude that, where he is concerned, life and death are completely beyond his influence and control. Whereby, man becomes gullible to satan's evil plan of self-destruction. Man views as normal satan's promulgated distortions: life (65 - 70 years); health (must die from something); death (it's inevitable). Consequently, he makes no effort to live forever, maintain perfect health and win the victory over the not-so-natural death, the evil by-product of sin.

The teachings of Euro-gentile institutions, both educational and theological, always strengthen the hand of the iniquitous. Is that a strange phenomenon? Not to the Sons and Daughters of God. The deceptively inspired thinking pattern - that death is unpreventable - gives great impetus to the cigarette smoker and manufacturer, the alcohol drinker and distiller, the carnivorous man and the slaughterhouse. This thinking pattern has man believing that regardless of whatever effort man makes, death is still going to occur. He never once considers that with so many thousands of built-in factors to enhance and hasten his death, that they are all a part of a diabolical plot or plan against him. He should bear in mind that since the "surely die" syndrome has engrossed his present society, he should contemplate uprooting himself and relocating elsewhere. And if at this present time he does not know of a suitable location, then he should search for a place where he will not be endowed by so many death-enhancing factors.

> *"By faith Abraham, when he was called to go out into a place which he should after receive for an inheritance, obeyed; and he went out, not knowing where he went.*
>
> *By faith he sojourned in the land of promise, as in a strange country, dwelling in tabernacles with Isaac and Jacob, the heirs with him of the same promise;*
>
> *For he looked for a city which hath foundations, whose builder and maker is God."*

Hebrews 11:8-10

There has never been a time in history when men did so many obvious things to destroy themselves. Man today is the major contributor to his own death and disease-ridden body. It is simple to determine that an awesome evil force is hidden somewhere in the control room (mind). Man has made a daily routine of committing suicide as if he has no self-control. If self-destruction was the rare exception, we could possibly consider it a far-out, odd, periodic mad occurrence. But it seems to me the whole world has been deceived. All components, government, institutions and people are drunk and so obviously craving degeneracy.

Yet, as strange as it may seem, in no country on this planet is there an active comprehensive war going on against death. However, there is a definite government-sponsored, institutionalized war (albeit subtle) against life. The devil has caused great fear to enter our hearts at the slightest thought of death. He is invincible, the undisputed champion in the confrontation with life.

When profoundly considered, if death cannot be defeated, then neither can we defeat satan, for our introduction to death came through him. Thus it becomes apparent that it is satan who has promulgated the erroneous doctrine of "death's superiority." It is his evil spirit that continues the "you don't have a chance to win" dogma. It is evident that that's his battle strategy. His tactics have worked perfectly; you offer little or no resistance. It has reached the point where television advertisements encourage you to secure your burial plot and make your funeral arrangements "ahead of time." The agents of death are everywhere. You are unarmed, unprepared, lost, confused, and naively insouciant before the phalanx representing death's interests. However, we are taught by the prophets of God that death will be defeated.

"And he will destroy in this mountain the face of the covering cast over all people, and the veil that is spread over all nations.

He will swallow up death in victory; and the Lord God will wipe away tears from all faces; and the rebuke of his people shall he take away from all the earth; for the Lord hath spoken it."

Isaiah 25:7-8

Death, then, is moved by God from the unknown to the known, from the invisible to the visible, and becomes something tangible: something to be seen, comprehended, engaged in some manner of Divine combat and subsequently defeated. To defeat something requires planning, strategy and tenacity, but more than that, the one you're fighting against has to be identifiable.

Though the inhabitants of the earth do dwell under the shadow of death, salvation is nigh at hand, for unknown to you, the war has already begun in a little mustard seed called "The Kingdom of God." The war began with the resurrection of the "God Mind" to bring new understanding to the people of the earth concerning God, the devil, good, evil, health, sickness, life and death. My message of truth is to emphasize that if we are still dying it is a direct result of something we still do not know. Lack of knowledge causes us to do things we should not; we die as a result of things we did when we did not know. Death is therefore relative to a low level of intellect.

131

Death in itself is tragic evidence that man has fallen into a state of confusion and weakness. For example, the government does not have the strength to refuse the licensing of the manufacture of cigarettes. The manufacturer is too weak to stop production; the victim is un-equipped to stop buying and smoking. The people are incapable of justifying the necessity of a smoke-free environment. Thus weakness prevails, and so does death.

Now the adversary, the same one that prescribed your present lifestyle and caused you to take umbrage at my prior calls for a return to dietary sanity, is attempting to seize the initiative. He is recom-mending a physical change of lifestyle. With the dissemination of such information, he overtly appears concerned about your health. You forget that he promised you health and prosperity, not infirmities when you embarked with him on this tragic journey. Nevertheless, his dissemination of supposedly good health information will have a debilitating effect on your future. I accept the consequences of in-forming you that it is another satanic good and evil plot and deception.

To be perfectly candid, I must convey to you that "faith without works is dead being alone." All change for those truly in search of better health begins with a change of spirit with the renewal of a strong relationship with God. If there is no spiritual change, the dietary change alone will be futile. That is not to imply that you won't experience some superficial improvement. However it will definitely not be the change from dying to living. The total positive dietary effects can only be attained by a renewed relationship with God.

Let us consider the familiar apple, long held to "keep the doctor away." The prerequisite to receiving the real benefits from the real apple is that you must have an obedient spirit to the real God. Believe me, this is truth, and no matter how fastidious your eating habits may become, or how hard you try, you won't be able to circumvent lawful principles compounded in the apple. The apple has come forth from the same soil that yielded you, not of its own accord, but in accordance with the command of Genesis. The apples weren't brought forth haphazardly, but as part of a Divine order and cycle; they are not just to nourish anything or just anybody, but a special God-creation. It is only capable of yielding its nourishment to one of similar character or spirit. It possesses a certain chemistry that was pre-determined by God. The apple is obedient only to God; it has no double mind (good and evil). It is bound to perform only within the framework for which it was created.

The seeds were commanded to bring forth their own kind. This command links them together with the individual unto whom they were to provide the fundamental nutrients. They are restricted from yielding their valuable, life-giving substance except to a specific creation that is of their kind and likeness, or likened unto God. Certainly we can understand this to be the fundamental requirement of a God that had fashioned a specific being and instructed him as to what he should consume. Most definitely in his infinite wisdom he has instructed these plants as to what they should yield and to whom. The nutritional value of a God-created apple provided to a righteous man is inevitably greater than to the wicked, whereas a hybrid or genetically-tampered (non-God-made) food such as a seedless watermelon, grape or nectarine would greater sustain the wicked.

Aren't you aware that you must plant the right seed for the proper yield? An orange seed will not provide the nourishment or the yield of apples. The earth only responds to the proper seed content or seed chemistry. This would certainly verify that the soil of the earth is highly intelligent insomuch that it will not yield its increase to a hostile spirit. That means that the present world system isn't getting the desired or required nutritional benefits from the yield of the soil. If a plant is a living organism, doesn't it seem logical that they would react differently in a dead organism? Somehow, then, they must have a form of intelligence to discern the difference.

> *"And I will make them and the places round about my hill a blessing, and I will cause the shower to come down in his season; there shall be showers of blessing.*
>
> *And the tree of the field shall yield her fruit, and the earth shall yield her increase, and they shall be safe in their land, and shall know that I am the Lord, when I have broken the bands of their yoke, and delivered them out of the hand of those that served themselves of them."*

*"And I will raise up for them a plant of renown, and they shall be
no more consumed with hunger in the land, neither bear the
shame of the heathen any more."*

Ezekiel 34:26-27, 29

When a certain vitamin or mineral is missing, the metabolism is
affected. Can we understand truthfully the chemistry of iron refusing
to be absorbed without folic acid and Vitamin C, yet not understand
God and truth being vital to the metabolism of life-giving, life-sustaining nourishment from plants? I make note of a statement by Dr.
Lawrence S. Kubie, outstanding authority in the field of psychiatry
and psychoanalysis:

*"It is literally true that no man has ever used more than a small
fragment of his brain power. In fact, even the most alert of us are never
wholly awake, much less fully in action...Why is this? It is because the
brain's psychological products are so organized that almost from birth we
are continuously blocked by conflicts among internal factions. This has
been man's lot from the days of Adam until this moment; yet it is specifically here that we stand on the threshold of a new kind of life. The future
opens up to us the possibility that we may learn to end the waste and
destructiveness of this internal impasse, freeing our enormous latent
creative powers from the crippling and paralyzing domination of uncon-
scious conflicts.*

*...The infinite creative potential of the human brain is housed in a
potentially indestructible body...which has a built-in replacement system,
its own self-replenishing devices! We have learned that as long as the
supply system is intact the body continuously takes itself apart and puts
itself together, not merely organ by organ, or cell by cell, but literally
molecule by molecule. Potentially, therefore, it is constantly renewed and
never ages. Consequently, there is no reason why any human being need
die.* [He cites some remaining problems to be overcome, medically, which
he is confident will soon be accomplished.] *Someday men and women will
stop dying, and will live forever."*

Little children, all flora and fauna have been given a form of
intelligence, all are required to function within pre-determined cycles
as commanded by the God of all living. Today's rulers of darkness
have become the creators of an artificial world, striving to coerce right
to submit to wrong. But the earth has stubbornly refused to yield to

those in opposition to God. The adversary of God does not desire to comply with the will of God, and has chosen to impose his will upon the creation through deception and artificiality. Because of great deception, the people have accepted a counterfeit concept of life and living. Their tongues are full of sin. They have artificial taste buds that desire lots of sugar, salt and other flavoring that give a false impression of goodness and only momentary satisfaction. Again, I'm saying simply that an apple will react differently in the stomach of someone hostile to God than it would in the stomach of one who has yielded to the cycles of God. No individual in opposition to God will ever taste or experience real life and living.

"Is there iniquity in my tongue? Cannot my taste discern perverse things?"

Job 6:30

"And God said, Let the earth bring forth vegetation, and herb yielding seed, and the fruit tree yielding fruit after his kind, whose seed is in itself, upon the earth: and it was so.

And the earth brought forth vegetation, and herb yielding seed after his kind, and the tree yielding fruit, whose seed was in itself, after his kind: and God saw that it was good."

"And God said, Behold, I have given you every herb bearing seed, which is upon the face of all the earth, and every tree, in which is the fruit of a tree yielding seed; to you it shall be for meat."

Genesis 1:11-12, 29

Be circumspect when reading the preceding scriptural references. God brought forth plant life and gave it reproductive power through seeds. These seeds were to produce continuously after their kind. They were established to exist eternally, so long as they remained non-resistant to God's Plan. Man too, was given the same kind of procreative seed and instructed to eat after his kind, plants with seed life. As plants were grown from the same soil from which he was created, they were likened as a part of his family. The responsibility to oversee the growth and development of all plants was put into his hands, and likewise for his growth and development in their hands.

135

Doesn't it seem logical and so perfectly Holy that man, whose life depends upon a seed, should consume plants from the soil which created him? Do you think or assume that a seedless grape or watermelon will have the same nutritional effect upon the man as a grape or watermelon with seeds? Isn't there something essential that the seed furnishes to the pulp or meat of the fruit that has to be passed on to the seed of man? Would not the continuous consumption of foods that do not engender seeds produce a man in the same manner? Has an artificial seed yielded an artificial man with an artificial mind that now requires an artificial diet and life? Consider this recent revelation concerning "seed vegetables" affirming that the original message of Genesis regarding dietary development was predicated upon a higher intellect which shared with man the secrets of living substances that were part of the living organs of his soul.

> *"In 1980 a National Research Council (NRC) committee of the National Academy of Sciences, commissioned by the National Cancer Institute (NCI), began summarizing current information on diet and cancer. By June 1982 the committee had found strong enough evidence to offer several interim dietary guidelines that are, it reports, 'both consistent with good nutritional practices and likely to reduce the risk of cancer.' Seed vegetables, those vegetables whose edible parts are seeds or tubers, dried beans, chickpeas, cereal grains, potatoes, for example - contain compounds that seem to intercept the activity of tumor promoters. In one experiment, feeding soybeans to a strain of rat that is highly susceptible to breast cancer greatly reduced the onset of breast tumors. In another, the skin of mice was painted with two compounds known to initiate and to promote cancer - but the cancer process was delayed and the number of tumors was significantly lower in the animals fed soybeans.*
>
> *Because most people eat some seed vegetables every day, Troll believes that protection is probably a matter of quantity consumed. The NRC recommends increasing consumption of these and other vegetables along with whole-grain cereals and fruit in the daily diet."*

"At Last An Anti-Cancer Diet"
Walter S. Ross, <u>Readers Digest</u>, February 1983.

Are we with eyes to see beholding a spurious world? Is democracy really a progressive social system or a hell disguised as heaven and bliss? Are the earth's inhabitants transposed sons and daughters of satan instead of sons and daughters of God? Does true love and worship of God exist or the love and worship of the devil? Is a primary concern of man to make real friends or real money? Is the planet seen through the eyes of God or the boardrooms of big business? How could a people that were really smart allow someone to destroy the earth's eco-systems? Could you imagine an individual with truly higher education not knowing the difference between something as obvious as heaven and hell?

As a matter of fact, nothing seems authentic anymore, no real men, no genuine women, no bona fide children or families. This is the reason that there has to be a new world, a return to the image and likeness of God. You are as one that is dead to the truth about his life and life in general. You have lost the eternal power of renewal and health which were once a fundamental part of your true God image and likeness. The problem is either a lack of the spiritual insight required to discern or the spiritual strength required to make the changes needed once you do discern. The struggle has to take on a new dimension: a spiritual and Godly dimension. It has to be led by men being led by God. Leadership is the key. With Moses and the Levites in the wilderness, the problem was: "You, (Moses), take too much upon yourself seeing we are all Holy." Blinded by jealousy, arrogance and err they became oblivious. They were unaware that their Holiness had to be derived from the Plan given to Moses by God. They had to accept him in order to find their acceptance. It was the same with Elijah and Ahab, and Yeshua and the Sanhedrin.

Your present leaders are operating within the parameters of this evil system; they are impotent. Subsequently, for the sake of their livelihood, they must keep you involved in the system to which they are accountable. So they led you into the trap as a matter of necessity. Accordingly, if the struggle for true freedom is to succeed, it must definitely be guided by those who have overcome the impediment of the system.

Yeshua said "I am not of this world." He spoke of another world (system), taking individuals out of one world and into another, telling even those who were considered successful, "you must be born again." There are solutions, attainable solutions, to your problems. But the solution will place you in opposition to the present irreverent world system which governs the underworld. Because of intimidation and deception, you continue to choose darkness instead of light, or wrong instead of right. It is deceptive for you to think that the problems of my/our people are insurmountable. There are men that know how to heal your ailments and infirmities and keep you healthy; to keep the men out of jail; to return the feminine nature to women, children to childhood and parents to the task of mending the family structure; to bring peace and everlasting joy into your lives.

But can there be a change of substance (physical evironment) without a change of thought (spiritual environment)? Again, we find ourselves being cast back to square one: leadership. The only solution is leadership anointed and sent by God - the kind of leadership that you've been rejecting since your fall into oblivion.

> *"And this is the condemnation, that light is come into the world, and men loved darkness rather than light, because their deeds were evil.*
>
> *For everyone that doeth evil hateth the light, neither cometh to the light, lest his deeds should be reproved.*
>
> *But he that doeth truth cometh to the light, that his deeds may be manifest, that they are wrought in God."*
>
> **John 3:19-21**
>
> *"Nevertheless they were disobedient, and rebelled against thee, and cast thy law behind their backs, and slew the prophets which testified against them to turn them to thee, and they wrought great provocations."*
>
> **Nehemiah 9:26**
>
> *"In vain have I smitten your children; they received no correction. Your own sword hath devoured your prophets, like a destroying lion."*
>
> **Jeremiah 2:30**

Noah knew how to save you. Likewise did Moses, the prophets, Yeshua and many others too numerous to mention. Again I beseech you to understand that my mention of men of God bear no reference to apostate religion. Religion is part of the system, the pacifier. Most of your contemporary leaders are, or have been, ministers. Certainly, Black leaders are included in this prognosis. When I say God, you automatically think religion and become defensive, and in many instances, outright hostile. In America alone, there are more than 2,000 religious denominations which exist solely because of religion's ability to maintain a cloak of darkness over the inhabitants. Apostate religion is condoned not because it is succeeding, but because it is failing. Religion is of this world; righteousness is of the new world.

Let us consider as we reflect back to the creation. For the overwhelming majority of the last six million or six thousand years - whichever is your doctrinal perspective and numerical preference - the human family remained agrarian. It had mainly remained intact through genius and dynasty, wonders and miracles and great institutions of learning. Was this by plan, coincidence or necessity? Then suddenly came a dominion unlike any that preceded it: men of evil ambition and bent on defying God and His creations, attempting to disprove His creative truth while neutralizing His authority. This dominion took man away from the soil, his genesis. Euro-gentiles have very subtly disconnected man from nature to the extent that he reads the notification of the earth being an "endangered species" without anger and without alarm.

What kind of future has been/is being prepared for you as a result of the use of "bio-technology?"

"Genetic engineering, specifically recombinant DNA, is a radical new technological development, one that allows traditional boundaries between dissimilar species to be broken down, and the genetic code of living organisms to be permanently altered. Already being field tested are biotechnology food crops with never-before-seen genetic combinations: cantaloupe and yellow squash containing genes from bacteria and virus; potatoes with chicken and waxmoth genes; tomatoes with flounder and tobacco genes; corn with firefly genes; rice with pea genes.

Researchers are already predicting that within our lifetime, genetically engineered food production will eliminate farming as we've known it.

139

Agriculture will move off the soil and into biosynthetic industrial processes controlled by biotech companies and corporate giants like Monsanto, Upjohn and others." *

Waxmoth = a species of the moth insect.

Flounder = a species of fish

Less than 100 years ago all of the earth's inhabitants maintained lifestyles which kept them in close contact or proximity with the four principal elements associated with life: fire (sun), earth (soil), air and water. Now the fire (sun) without the ozone has become our enemy. We are now told that to walk in it is like walking on a tightrope. Don't sit in the sun for long and definitely don't lie down under her once healthful rays. Do you recall not so long ago being told of the benefits of sunshine: "Be sure to get plenty of sunshine!" Now we are confined to observing its beauty on television during our daily 10 hour stint of duty in front of the set. In addition, we have gas masks being worn in Thailand and severe air pollution alerts in Los Angeles and Mexico City. Then there is acid rain, polluted water and dangerous beaches closed to bathers. The elements are gone and you think you're really living! As a matter of fact, those that govern you have coined a suitable, pacifying misnomer for your sick mind: they simply call it an "alternative lifestyle."

Your vital interaction with the elements was/is connected with your existence on this planet. For instance, most pharmaceutical medicines are vain attempts to imitate the healing properties found in plants. Scientists are stalking the last remnants of the earth's rain forests and tropical regions in search of cures for the ailments afflicting man today. These scientists are studying what appears to be simple botany. But unknown to you, they are in search of the earth's properties for sustaining life everlasting. They are trying to find the keys to man's life which they know are found in plants. Once they accomplish their goal, they feel they can give and/or take life. They will then expect to assume the title of creator, God, the giver of life. While the

Source: Communicator, Newsletter of the Organic Crop Improvement Association (International) Inc. January 1993. Written by Dianne Joy Goodman: West Coast Director, Pure Food Campaign and Ted L. Howard: Director Pure Food Campaign.

laymen's search for life and good health is directed to the rib joint, the hot dog stand, Kentucky Fried Chicken and giant hamburgers, the upper eschelon are researching plants and soil.

I recall a study many years ago, in which researchers monitored plants (through measurable electrochemical impulses) during a series of interactions with humans. One encounter involved a man applying a flame to the underside of a plant's leaf, which set off a torrent of distress signals. Later, when the same man reentered the laboratory room, monitoring instruments nearly went haywire in registering a response! We've all known individuals who possessed "green thumbs." Botanists uphold those who talk to their houseplants, suggesting that they thrive in a happy home environment and respond positively to positive words and thoughts. The idea of an "intelligent" plant is not so far-fetched at all when we consider the intrinsic link between man and the creations. Clearly all species of fauna and flora possess an intelligence that man has ignorantly and arrogantly dismissed.

Doesn't it seem feasible to you that man has to be eternally connected to the soil from which he came? Perhaps shelling peas, snapping beans, picking greens and shucking corn are spiritually important acts with benefits far beyond essential nutrition. What is the stimulus that has led us to this point in history where there are whole generations of youth that cannot comprehend the God element in food? They know only the junk foods and attractive supermarket shelves. What kind of nutrition does an intelligent plant provide to a young daughter that is ashamed to be seen touching its stem and rinsing its leaves? Or how does a pea feel about a young man embarrassed at putting it into a bushel? Was it a lack of progress by our fathers that kept the entire community in some way involved in planting and/or harvesting?

In ancient African/Edenic cultures, planting and harvesting were seasons of feasting and praising God. In many cultures, such as the African/Edenic Hebrews, there were Holy days set aside to sanctify the first fruit of the harvest. These first fruits of the harvest had to be brought to the Levites and waved or lifted up before God. A form of thanksgiving had to be presented before God before any consumption was allowed. It appears that plants were given a very high honor and respect in the ancient societies. Was this a vain ritual or a valuable reminder of the strong eternal bond that exists between man and his kind: e.g. plant substances that can combine to maintain and recreate man's cells, bones, blood, etc.? As a matter of fact, it is more reasonable to say, that there is a combination of plants that can create an entirely new man after their kind. When an individual comprehends that true life is intrinsically tied to the soil and plants, then he will better understand how the festive seasons of the ancients paid homage to the beauty, splendor, glory and power of plants or God's pro-creative power given to plants.

What is actually taking place and why is it absolutely necessary to pray a prayer of thanksgiving before the consumption of food (not animal products or by-products)? Does this prayer (over plant life) affect the biological processes of digestion and metabolism? Is this prayer being made as a necessity unto God or does it activate the biological clock to prepare proper physiological responses.

"Ye shall keep my statutes. Thou shalt not let thy cattle gender with a diverse kind: thou shalt not sow thy field with mingled seed: neither shall a garment mingled of linen and woollen come upon thee."

Leviticus 19:19

"And when ye shall come into the land, and shall have planted all manner of trees for food, then ye shall count the fruit thereof as uncircumcised: three years shall it be as uncircumcised unto you: it shall not be eaten of.

But in the fourth year all the fruit thereof shall be holy to praise the Lord withal.

And in the fifth year shall ye eat of the fruit thereof, that it may yield unto you the increase thereof: I am the Lord your God."

Leviticus 19:23-25

"Thou shalt not sow thy vineyard with various seeds: lest the fruit of thy seed which thou hast sown, and the fruit of thy vineyard, be defiled."

Deuteronomy 22:9

Library shelves are replete with books about horticulture, but few to none make mention of the laws of God that must be taken into consideration in Divine Agriculture. The Euro-gentile dominion to its own hurt did embark upon the course of trying to outsmart God. Their genetic mutation and hybridization of plants has had far reaching ramifications that touch upon the very fabric of man's life, health and environment.

The above-mentioned scriptural references go far beyond planting and harvesting within the geographical boundaries of the land of Israel. These verses take into consideration that the life of man was well planned and interwoven with certain inalienable laws of nature. Is it by chance or the violation of the these laws that the Euro-centric world's food choices (agriculture, animal husbandry) account for a multiplicity of infirmities including the major portion of heart disease, and more than one-half of all cancers. In addition, their very congruous medical research is directed at treating the consequence of lifestyle factors rather than addressing the lifestyles itself. Subsequently, though modern medicine deceitfully boasts of having extended life spans, contemporary humanity's longevity falls dismally short of those found in the Old Testament and other ancient records. The logical question is simply: What is affected by the violation of these laws for planting of seed and mis-consumption of the fruit (food) of the trees? You must certainly be of the realization that something (the soil) or someone, or both are in some way negatively affected.

The failure of man to acknowledge that plant life has a high form of intelligence that it provides only to its kind shows a severe lack of intelligence on his part. Any person who does not ocasionally walk in or work in the soil is missing something. A field of mature watermelons is a wonder to behold. When you see one and comprehend its wonder, it will provide essential God knowledge for your

143

mind even before it provides the nourishment for your soul. Maybe one day soon, through the grace of God you will realize that plants are an inextricable part of the authentic life designed for all who honor and give reverence to God.

God is absolute; truth, the word of God is absolute; life is absolute; there should be no death during a lifetime. To live is to pursue God; to enjoy life is to enjoy serving God. Death comes into play only after man turns aside from the path of life. The tree of life is significant only if man eats of the tree of good and evil, after which it would become the goal of those seeking life. It also symbolizes the fact that the fruit of immortality (wisdom) will become available again unto man. Man cannot live and die. You cannot serve two masters - life and death. Death is not a part of life, neither is life a part of death. In Divine Hebraic thought you never prepare to die; you prepare to live. You are forever trying to establish, maintain and strengthen a connection with the eternal spirit which brings eternal life. This spirit transcends death.

After the fall away from life, man entered the process of death. Although he had fallen into the cycle of death, he did not immediately disappear from sight; he remained a corporeal being. After the fall of the Sons of Light, the spiritual Magna Carta was passed to the sons of darkness. It was significant that the fallen Sons of God came under the rule of the blind sons of darkness. When the blind lead the blind, they all fall into the pit. Since all things are relevant, an evil force came into existence called satan, the devil. He was made necessary by the law of relativity. The fool that desires to remain a fool has to be led by a fool. The Sons of Light, with eyes to see, could not mislead; therefore those desiring to be misled have to come under the guidance of a relevant spirit. Yeshua said "my sheep can hear my voice." All sheep hear the voice of their shepherd, for good or for evil. Those that cannot amalgamate or unite, must separate. That holds true in corporeal, as well as spiritual law. The righteous cannot remain in hell; neither can the wicked remain in heaven. We have been taught by the prophets of God that when evil rebelled against right, it was cast down from heaven. The forces of evil found no comfort in heaven.

"And the Lord God formed man of the dust of the ground, and breathed into his nostrils the breath of life; and man became a living soul."

Genesis 2:7

"What if ye shall see the Son of man ascend up where he was before?

It is the spirit that quickeneth; the flesh profiteth nothing: the words that I speak unto you, they are spirit, and they are life."

John 6:62-63

"For as the body without the spirit is dead, so faith without works is dead also."

James 2:26

When the God of creation breathed the breath of life into Adam he became a living soul, the product or creation of a living God. We can conclude without much difficulty that this "breath of life" was sense. And if it was given by God, we know of a certainty that it was God sense. He gave Adam a mind - the God mind. Can we also deduce that this act represents the presence of God on earth in the body or form of man? What was given to Adam? Was he created by God to represent the devil? What is the message that is being conveyed to the human family? We must be cognizant of the fact that life is equated with sense or God intellect. We find Yeshua in his ministry diligently stressing this same salient point. Yeshua is quoted as saying "It is the spirit that quickeneth" (giveth life). "The words (doctrines) that I speak (teach) to you are life, for the flesh profiteth nothing." God sense (intellect) is the principal element, the determining factor in man's existence and relationship with God.

It certainly stands to reason that if we are to maintain a close relationship with God, we must use His mind or intellect to govern our lives, build our cities, order our social structure, etc. Application of this mind would produce the highest form of life, a "heavenly" existence or an existence in heaven or paradise. God is universally connected with that which is above, or something high and exalted. Some kind of an ascension is always guaranteed when God is posi-

145

tively involved. From all indications, if we had kept and used our God sense we would have been governed by God - or by men governed by God - in a high, elevated, exalted place called heaven on this planet that He made to be inhabited by us.

It is relatively easy to grasp that the loss of the God-mind would cause a transition, decline or descent to a very low form of existence that can be equated with the opposite of life, even death. This existence must be defined as adversarial, or in opposition to God. The positive action of the God-mind creates heaven on earth. In contrast, a mind devoid of God certainly creates a hell on earth, or a very low form of existence.

Consider the <u>Webster's New Collegiate Dictionary's</u> definition of "underworld:" "The place of departed souls; hades (hell), a social sphere below the level of ordinary life, especially the world of organized crime." Paraphrasing the above-mentioned definition could assist greatly in the broadening of your creative understanding. For example, "the underworld" is the place wherein they that have departed from God's sacred way of life gather. Having departed from God, they now dwell in a base social environment far below Godly expectations and the former ordinary life. They are a well-trained, organized element in opposition to God, His people and creations. Remember, the devil is the master of deception. He has to make wrong appear right, darkness to appear as light and hell to appear as the "chosen milieu."

The ultimate objective of satan is to create a desire within you to do the things that are harmful and destructive to you. The purpose of my struggle to save your life is seen and felt in my constant plea to you to resist the devil and discontinue your involvement in his enticing but destructive trappings. Fast foods are usually attractive, time-saving, tasty, cheap, but very deadly, even suicidal. For example, I tell you to change your diet and abstain from meat. I'm aware that "Big Macs" taste good to you and so does Kentucky Fried Chicken and southern barbecued ribs. I'm aware that uni-sex clothing can be worn by both men and women, saving you closet space and income. Your subsequent involvement in committing obvious crimes against life demonstrates your nonchalant attitude about God and His judgment.

Then it is foolish to think that there should be no penalty for outright disregard for Divine Law. The Law and inspired writings of the prophets have high ethical requirements. They are neither cruel nor distressful. We must proceed forward with all deliberate speed to reinstitute their high precepts in the midst of the people. We shall mobilize them in our war against sin and rebellion, which constitute the present barrier between the earth's inhabitants and God.

To divert attention from the broader aspects of the underworld, the Euro-gentile and Euro-American define the criminal segment of their society as the "underworld." You are not vigilant, but naive and gullible. It does not require a lot of effort to deflect your concentration from the world's chief criminals to the microcosmic element labelled organized crime (underworld). The chief criminals have hoodwinked the people into believing that the underworld is the principal problem; uproot it and the problem of crime will be solved. You are deceived because you have eyes that cannot see, ears that cannot hear, and a mind that can't put it all together due to a lack of knowledge of the nature of the God that created you.

You are very familiar with the deceptive little cliche "be good or you're going to die and go to hell." It's been quoted in the midst of our people so long until they believe it to be the truth. Today in the Kingdom of God, we have exposed the lie, but guiding you through this maze of lies back unto God and sanity is very complex. I can assure you that you've already died and gone to hell! It may sound somewhat far-fetched from what you have been religiously taught, but it is the truth. Except for a very small confluence of spiritual men that have been preserved by God, the whole of the human family has been deceived. They have died and gone to hell and now dwell in the "underworld."

Consider these common news capsules from the "underworld:"

Sex and Booze Turn Hill into a School for Scandal
For years, Capitol Hill has been awash with rumors and allegations of sexual affairs and drunkenness by both senators and members of the House.

For example, Sen. Edward Kennedy, Massachusetts Democrat,

who has a widely known reputation as a womanizer, was discovered during a fall 1987 lunch having sexual intercourse with a woman on the floor of a private dining room at La Brasserie, a popular Capitol Hill restaurant, according to sources familiar with the incident. In 1981, Rep. Jon Hinson, Mississippi Republican, resigned from Congress after he was found performing oral sex on a male clerk in a restroom in the House office building. (**The Washington Times,** **March 2, 1989**)

"Brothers Loving Brothers" (an excerpt from a handout designed for the Black Community in Washington, D.C.)

"The virus which causes AIDS lives in blood and semen. To keep the virus outside of you, you must keep other people's blood and semen outside of your body. That's what safer sex is: sex which keeps other people's blood and semen out of your body.

Have fun, but don't get caught in the heat of passion.

Holding and hugging, cuddling and nibbling, masturbation and rubbing bodies together are several ways to express your love. Blood and semen don't usually get inside your body when you do these things. Love your brother, and love him safely!" (**Spectrum,** **AIDS Education to the Black Community, Washington, D.C.**)

The Devil's Disciple, The Pitiless Predator

Dodd found a four-year old boy playing alone in an elementary school playground. He coaxed Lee Iseli home with him to play some games. "When we got there, I told him he had to be real quiet because my neighbor lady didn't like kids." Dodd said. He then stripped off Lee Iseli's clothes, tied the boy to the bed and began taking pictures as he molested the child. He later mounted the photos in a 10-cm-by-150-cm pink photo album labeled Family Memories. He paused at one point to make an entry in his diary: "6:30 p.m. Will probably wait until morning to kill him. That way his body will still be fairly fresh for experiments after work." Dodd began strangling the boy at 5:30 a.m. he revived the child twice before finally killing him and hanging the body in a closet and burning the boy's clothing, except the Ghostbusters underpants, which he kept as a trophy (**Time, January 11, 1993**)

The Fatal Triangle: Crack and Syphilis Spread AIDS Among the Poor: Sexual Binges

People who frequent crack houses, new data show, are increasingly being infected with syphilis and are testing positive for AIDS. In crack houses, men and women engage in extremely high levels of sexual activity, often with many partners, psychiatrists who treat addicts say. Dr. Carol J. Weiss, psychiatrist drug treatment expert at Cornell University Medical College, said that crack, unlike heroin and other drugs, often cause users to engage in binges of hyperactive sexual behavior. With larger doses of cocaine or crack, addicts are sexually aroused but cannot achieve orgasm; they may engage in sexual intercourse or masturbation for hours, often with many partners. In addition, women in crack houses often trade oral sex for drugs. (**The New York Times,** August 20, 1989)

Discovery of Heads Points to US Black Market in Body Parts

The discovery of five human heads in a parcel being shipped from here to Denver is one of several recent indications that an underground market may be developing for human organs and cadavers, some medical and legal authorities say. Many medical institutions report growing difficulty in obtaining organs and tissue needed for teaching and research.
(**Intl. Herald Tribune**, Sept. 26, 1986)

Trading Places, World's First...

Chinese surgeons have performed what is believed to be the world's first direct sex swap, exchanging internal sexual organs between a man and a woman, neither of whom know each other. Doctors say a 22-year old woman received the testicles of a 30-year-old man, who received her ovaries during operations last week. Doctors constructed a false penis for the woman from her stomach lining. They replaced the man's penis with a vagina made of leather. Further operations are necessary for the ex-woman to have a male erection but doctors are confident the ex-man would be able to have a complete sex life. Neither patient will be able to procreate. (**USA Today,** Friday July 24, 1992)

(Abortion) Murdered for Cosmetics

Once an unborn baby has been deliberately killed (aborted) in the womb of its mother, its tissues, organs, etc., etc., are now being put to commercial use. The substance found in connective tissue, bone and cartilage, is widely used in cosmetics, but is usually of animal origin. However, certain evidence suggests that this collagen could be taken from fetal material. The sale of late term elective abortions at D.C. General Hospital in America brought $68,000 between the years of 1966 to 1976. One abortionist states, "a baby is becoming property. We kill, keep and sell the property." (**Muslim Journal**)

It's a Boy, Says Male Mother-to-be

Malaybalay, Philippines, 32-year-old Filipino male nurse who is six months pregnant is expecting a boy and says he already feels the baby kicking inside him. The pregnant man, whose real name has not been made public but who has been given the nickname "Carlo," is a hermaphrodite who says he was born with male and female sexual organs. "I feel proud that I'm going to be the mother of a baby boy. I'm happy that now I'm really feeling fulfilled like a complete woman," he said.
(**The Royal Gazette,** May 28, 1992)

The Straight Dope: Gerbil Stuffing?

The principle is simple: A tube is inserted in the rectum, and a recently manicured gerbil is induced to run up the tube and burrow in. There's some difference of opinion about what happens next. Some say gerbil somehow winds up in a bag or sack (perhaps a condom). Others say no sack is used - the gerbil simply squirms around eventually suffocates and is later eliminated during defecation. The key supposedly in the sensation of fur. Complaints often occur. Often the rectum/or anus becomes lacerated, torn, or infected. (The Manhattan publication "New York Talk" reported about a year ago that New York doctors first caught on to stuffing when they started encountering patients with infections previously found only in rodents). (NOTE: Upon further investigation the author says while numerous tales abound, he found no written record of stuffing.) (**The Chicago Reader,** 1988)

Waiter, There's a Rat in My Soup, And It's Delicious!

A Restaurant in China Serves Rat 30 Different Ways; We suggest the Kabobs - Guangzhou, China

The Cantonese people of south China are legendary for eating anything that moves - and some things that are still moving. The food market here features cats, raccoons, owls, doves and snakes along with bear and tiger's paw, dried deer penis and decomposed monkey skeletons. Now China's first restaurant dedicated to serving rat. That's right: Rat. Rat with Chestnut and Duck. Lemon Deep Fried Rat. Sauteed Rat Slices with Vermicelli. In fact, the menu lists 30 different rat dishes, even including Liquored Rat Flambe, along with more mundane dishes such as Hot Peppers Silkworm, Raccoon with Winter Melon and Sliced Snake and Celery. And in the six months since the doors opened, customers have been scampering in at all hours to the euphemistically named Jialu (Super Deer) Restaurant. **(The Wall Street Journal, May 31, 1991)**

Scouting's Sex Abuse Trail Leads To 50 States

For parents, the local Boy Scout troop is a safe place to send the kids. For child molesters, it's an ideal place to meet them. The result: on an average of more than once a week for the past two decades, the Cub Scouts, Boy Scouts or Explorer has reported being sexually abused by a Scout leader. An investigation by the Washington Times shows that at least 1,151 Scouts have reported being abused by their leaders over the past 19 years, making sex abuse more common in Scouting than accidental deaths and serious injuries combined. **(The Washington Times, May 20, 1991)**

Unsettling Report on an Epidemic of Rape

The statistics are horrifying enough to make a mother rush her daughter into hiding -- and perhaps join them. According to a federally funded survey published by the National Victim Center last week, 683,000 adult women were forcibly raped in the U.S. in 1990. That figure is five times the number of sexual assaults reported by the Justice Department for the same year... The survey authors estimated that more than 12 million American women have been raped at least once in their life, but the true shocker is that 61% of rape victims were younger than 18 at the time of their attack. Three out of 10 had not yet reached their 11th birthday. In almost 80% of the cases, the women knew their rapist. ... only 16% of the assaults are reported. **(Time, May 4, 1992)**

Child Prostitution Spreads, Partly Because of AIDS Fears

Brussels - Doctors, police officers and social workers accustomed to dealing with sexual abuse are reporting that children and adolescents are increasingly in demand as prostitutes because clients see them as "safer" and likely to be free of AIDS .

In the brothels of Manila and Bangkok, the port district of Rio de Janeiro and the back rooms of Frankfurt, pimps hawk the services of children as young as 8 to 13 years old by emphasizing that they are "clean," experts said at the Unesco conference here on "the sex trade and human rights." So there is a high price on virginity. The procurers are going after children 10 or 11 or 12 years old." **(International Herald Tribune, April 10-11, 1993)**

Terror Stalks the Nation's Capital, Gunman Takes Aim at Anyone

Eight random, sometimes deadly drive-by shotgun attacks on pedestrians in two neighborhoods are terrorizing residents and frustrating police. The gunman, who is believed to drive a blue or green Toyota Tercel, strikes at lone pedestrians without regard to race or sex. He uses a pump-action shotgun and fires at close range officials said. The attacks have become more brazen. In the most recent, the gunman chased one man, who escaped; shot at and missed another, who dived under a van and then shot and killed a third - all on the same street. "I don't walk the streets anymore," said Allan Edwards, 60. **(USA Today, April 13, 1993)**

****

Why do they classify the relatively few individuals involved in what is called "the world of organized crime" when the legal activities and crimes of government and business pose the greater threat and cause the most damage to both man and environment? The illegal traffic in drugs numbers hundreds of tons, while the legalized, "over-the-counter" traffic in harmful drugs totals millions of tons. The mob controls prostitution; the government turns a blind eye to prostitution. When the government apprehends companies selling products that are dangerous to your health, they then merely assist the guilty party in developing the foreign markets of unsuspecting victims and continue to traffic the lethal contraband. Clearly they are engaged in the illegal traffic of harmful substances.

Recently Holland's Parliament lowered the "age of consent" from 16 to 12! In addition to that, the law passed by a landslide vote of 145 to 5! Said a spokesman for the Justice Ministry: "We did not debate whether or not it is good for children to have sex at these ages, but we tried to protect the child more in the case where they are unwilling...We have received not a single complaint from the Dutch public." Dutch lawmakers and their constituents alike are members of the "underworld."

A man or woman may decide to legally undergo a sex change operation. God created them male and female in harmony with nature, and in total disregard to God's laws and statutes, they are transformed to androgynous mutations. In today's modern, democratic society, two men or two women "hook up," "fall" in love, proceed on to their neighborhood parish and get legally married. The first executive order sought by U.S. President, Bill Clinton, was to guarantee equal treatment of homosexuals in the military. Meanwhile, New York's school system debated the use of "Daddy's Roommate" (another male, of course) as a textbok for the city's kindergarten students. They discover D.D.T. is lethal to both land and man, so they export it to those that are not aware of the after-effects of dangerous chemicals. And, as in most instances in organized crime, the C.I.A. silences all opposition.

There is a world where orgies, wife-swapping and devil worship are constitutionally allowed, where the proliferation of evil is protected and thus encouraged. Journalists have a right to lie; manufacturers are allowed to lie and steal; children are exposed to too much too fast. The pages of this book are far too few to list the plethora of evil, law-breaking daily activities of the fallen souls. If those who violate man's laws and statutes can be called citizens of the underworld, certainly those who see through the eyes of God can see the broader aspect of this vast underworld through its democratic disguise. The former family of nations is in a snare. You don't just walk out of a trap. My principal objective in this composition is to give you the required mind, point you in the proper direction and lead you in the great escape.

> *"And I will make thee to pass with thine enemies into a land which thou knowest not; for a fire is kindled in mine anger, which shall burn upon you."*

Jeremiah 15:14

153

"Who is blind, but my servant? Or deaf, as my messenger that I sent? Who is blind as he that is perfect, and blind as the Lord's servant?

Seeing many things, but thou observest not; opening the ears, but he heareth not.

The Lord is well pleased for his righteousness' sake; he will magnify the law, and make it honorable.

But this is a people robbed and spoiled; they are all of them snared in holes, and they are hid in prison houses; they are for a prey, and none delivereth; for a spoil, and none saith, Restore.

Who among you will give ear to this? Who will hearken and hear for the time to come?

Who gave Jacob for a spoil, and Israel to the robbers? Did not the Lord, he against whom we have sinned? for they would not walk in his ways, neither were they obedient unto his law.

Therefore, he hath poured upon him the fury of his anger, and the strength of battle; and it hath set him on fire round about, yet he knew not; and it burned him, yet he laid it not to heart."

Isaiah 42:19-25

"Therefore my people are gone into captivity, because they have no knowledge; and their honorable men are famished, and their multitude dried up with thirst.

Therefore hell hath enlarged herself, and opened her mouth without measure; and their glory, and their multitude, and their pomp, and he that rejoiceth, shall descend into it."

Isaiah 5:13-14

The aforementioned scriptures clearly refer to the fallen Sons of Light who have turned aside from God. They have descended into the abode of those without God, into the land of His/their enemies, described as places where there is a continuous fire in which the people dwell. When the Sons of Light find themselves without God, they are also without God consciousness. The fire burns them and one associated with them, yet they are void of feeling (dead), and are unable to comprehend the relativity of their new surroundings. If as is written, fire can burn you continuously and you fail to react to the conflagration, you have no mind, no life. Death engulfs you.

The prophets saw in their vision a non-mythical, real, geographical hell on earth that opened her mouth without end to receive the fallen souls. It was a land or lands wherein the disposition and character of the inhabitant was adversarial to God, thus the land of an enemy of right. Those dead in God are buried in these lands, being tormented without end by fire. If they are ever to escape the horrors of hell, they must be resurrected. Life (truth/the word of God) has to be breathed into the dead, dry bones, causing them to spring up from their graves and into action for God.

Further on we find Yeshua saying if his doctrine is believed, an individual would never die, again equating life with some form of intellect or sense. He further passionately complained "Why do you not understand my speech (doctrine) and hear my words? He that is of God heareth God's words: you can't hear them because you are of your Father the devil." Again we see their inability to hear being attributed to their being possessed by some form of strange ungodly sense (intellect). This strange mind prevents their comprehension of truth, which is the breath of life that God breathed into Adam. They are imprisoned or trapped in hell.

Let us consider the present institutions of learning that have fashioned the minds of those in and of this present world system. We must first ask if there is a force on this planet that is in opposition to God and truth. We find our answer in the book of Genesis.

"And the serpent said unto the woman, Ye shall not surely die."

Genesis 3:4

Yeshua said satan was the "Father of a lie." The devil came on the scene prevaricating, and no doubt because of deviousness, he will meet his consummation. It's imperative that an individual whose total existence depends on or revolves around a lie, must maintain an educational system that opposes truth. Anyone indoctrinated with his teachings would find it difficult to understand and believe truth. As a matter of fact, those educated or trained by him would no doubt find it very easy to believe a lie or things that are extremely foolish.

How do sane people choose darkness over light? Wrong over right? It is educated into them; they are literally taught to make the wrong decisions. Satan, after disguising himself as an angel of light, moved expediently to institutionalize wrong. Organized evil is part of a legal system of government, and often hard to detect. After all, it has a legal, valid license. Once the devil moved into the educational system, the objective was simply to make truth hard to believe; right to appear as if it was way out in left field; God equated with the mere acceptance of a religion.

After a very successful dominion of deception, guess who's having the hardest time gaining acceptance in the minds of the people...those telling the truth! Guess what lifestyle seems ridiculous...the right one! And you'd never guess who's having a hard time gaining followers ...God! If you could use your imagination for a moment, consider an educational system under the control of satanic influence. Certainly it would offer some very basic courses, enticing careers and professional opportunities. But somewhere in the course of learning, the acceptance of evil by the student would have to be the institute's ultimate objective.

For example, I am hard pressed explaining that the ancient Egyptians who dwelled in an empire covering most of North Africa, Sudan, Ethiopia and Nubia, and were descendants of Ham, were Black. Yet with relative ease you can imagine British, French, Romans, Greeks, Germans and Scandinavians occupying these African lands three to four thousand years ago. I spend hours, days, weeks, months and years in the midst of intense debate with intellectually practical individuals that lie and refute a very easy-to-believe comprehensive truth. Why is it that the world citizens find it hard to believe that they should not consume animal flesh?

I also teach that homosexuality is an abomination before God and in the eyes of all Godly individuals. Those that condone such evil are the adversaries of God. They stand at the podiums and explain human rights, civil liberties and freedom of choice as the basis of their evil actions. Generally speaking, it appears to those with higher education that I am a threat to the pillar of democracy. I simply hold that a man was not intended by God to be penetrated anally by a penis; that his anus was created for the passage of waste from his body; that women are/were not given a penis to insert into another woman's vagina - simple truths that I thought were known to everyone. Now I'm portrayed as an extremist, someone way out in left field trying to coerce others with strange doctrine. And, of course, there's the current admonishments of those "progressive" minds who simply say "you'd better get with the 90's!" Who has trained intellects to justify evil and ungodliness?

Now the well-learned sociologists say that when a man approaches another male for sex, he should just politely say no if he doesn't consent. Politely say no?! Where in hell were they educated?! The nature of a real man causes anger to rise up in him at the thought of such a despicable act. The Godly must take a non-compromising, strong position against the ungodly. If not, you'll soon see the billboard and TV advertisements reminding men to avoid laxatives when going out for the evening. Thus, the difference between individuals or nations of people being led right or wrong, living or dying is sense, intellect. It all depends on whose mind you're using or better still, whose mind is using you.

"Hear, O heavens and give ear, O earth; for the Lord hath spoken: I have nourished and brought up children, and they have rebelled against me.

The ox knoweth his owner, and the ass, his master's crib, but Israel doth not know; my people doth not consider.

Ah, sinful nation, a people laden with iniquity, a seed of evildoers, children that are corrupters; they have forsaken the Lord, they have provoked the Holy One of Israel unto anger, they are gone away backward.

Why should ye be stricken any more? Ye will revolt more and more; the whole head is sick, and the whole heart faint.

157

From the sole of the foot even unto the head there is no soundness in it; but wounds, and bruises, and putrefying sores. They have not been closed, neither bound up, neither mollified with ointment."

Isaiah 1:2-6

We as a people must think our way out of this present predicament. In order to accomplish that, we must have another mind. Your present mind has been trained to keep you in the captivity. Only if we decide to do it God's way will He help. The principal questions subsequently become: How does God desire us to feel concerning those ruling over His creations? Should we feel that they've done a good job? What would God have us to do at this time in history? To be happy and just accept this world as it is? Should we even concern ourselves worrying about who is ruling the world? Should we be trying to get into this world or get out of it?

Truthfully, if this world could make us happy, we, too, would ask what need have we of God. You are in blind pursuit of the elusive "good life," a deceptive dream which is of course defined as a life of material accumulation and financial prosperity. Thus the evil Euro-gentile societies are correctly defined as the places to attain these things. Notwithstanding, the wealth of God is determined by the moral state of man, not the materialistic. These social systems block the world's pursuit and attainment of the real "good life:" oneness with God, His creations and people. There has to be a new beginning marking the end of our pursuit of the destructive American or Euro-centric dream.

You have been imprisoned so long in someone else's social system until you've become a victim of misfessance. Thoughts of what decisions you would make for yourself no longer even arouse your curiosity. Questions of war and peace, justices for the Supreme Court, inflation and recession, aid and grants, crime and punishment, apartheid or amalgamation are still majority decisions, not minority ones. On the truly sensitive issues, for genuine social change, you prefer not to rock the boat. For your own self-protection, you feel that on vital issues of national concern you must conform to the powers that be. You have chosen the burdens of slavery over the burdens of freedom.

After all, you are just too vulnerable a minority to place all of your accomplishments at risk, and besides, you can always safely hide behind the skirts of the 90% majority, disclaiming any real responsibility. Truthfully, as a minority people living with the permission of a host country, you are not empowered to make changes. That is the primary reason your homes are infested with dissension and your neighborhoods with crime, drugs, fear and disorder. Your present lifestyle serves the social needs of the majority. A land of our own, a neighborhood, a community, a city or state will provide us with the most profound choice of deciding our own destiny, of making genuine life and death decisions. In America, your command of choices concern only superficial issues; the difficult decisions are still being made for you by the slave master's descendants. You are now paranoid at even the thought of the responsibility of making the required decisions concerning your life, and suffering the criticisms and/or consequences of your choice.

This is an awesome choice that you will have to make when you decide to move from victim to victor. Sadly, many will find even the very real, ominous prospect of persecution in America to be preferable to the challenge of independence in another place with its attendant responsibility and accountability. You are in bondage to the will (ways) of your adversaries; they have shaped your daily life, and they control every aspect of your lives. You are trapped in the religion, education, politics and culture of an ungodly secular society. You are individualistic, materialistic pleasure seekers; you are dead in God. Your religious leaders are merely politicians in the pulpit vainly preaching love, unity and brotherhood, while in reality, not in support of the creation of an environment wherein they can be attained. Our enemies and friends are predetermined, predigested and prepackaged for us. We are/were given officially accepted and recognized religions. These Euro-gentile religions taught us who and what was proper to worship. By design and purpose, our adherence to European religious doctrines and political ideologies guarantee that we, as ex-slaves, will be without redemption and at the bottom of the ladder forever.

Within Euro-gentile religious institutions, the Black layman has been given only a token understanding of the true worship of God. The Black man's misunderstanding of the true worship of the Creator God is at the helm of his manifold problems. The ideologies and life aspirations of the Black church are basically those of his oppressor. Yet, the innate driving hunger to be satiated spiritually has caused them to partake and adopt any and every religion that passes their way.

In the beginning there was no religion given to our Fathers. They were given simply the keys to understanding the right way of life. When man was created in the image of God, he was also taught how to live in the environment he was placed. He was given a set of instructions. If they were followed, his life would have continuity; if he would not be obedient, he could not live.

The language of prophecy is clearly not synonymous with the language of contemporary Black theologians and religious leadership. Theodore D. Walker explores this idea in his work, Empower the People:

> "The biblical prophet, we recall, interprets the world in terms of relationship to God, and preaches a relentlessly God-conscious social ethic. The prophet describes the circumstance of the people in terms of the consequences of unrighteous behavior. The prophet predicts that if we continue in the ways of unrighteousness, our future and that of our descendants will be one of increased misfortune, suffering, and death - that is, 'the wages of sin.' And so the prophet prescribes that we should repent and take up the practice and habits of righteousness, of obedience to God's will, so as to contribute to the possibility of a more favorable future."

Through religious deception, man was convinced that disobedience to these natural laws and the universal order of his environment would not cause his death. The establishment of religion was/is the major obstacle being used to confuse man as to the original intent of the instructions of God. Now, more than ever before, the aversion to God's law is connected with religiosity. Contemporary society treats life as something the religiously pious attain after death; death has become as a mysterious journey to a distant place. Nevertheless,

160

in Genesis we are taught that life comes with sense - God sense. Religion is a satanic fabrication to discourage the search for the obtainable keys to life everlasting. Religion allows you to believe that you need only to confess your faith while nullifying your need for sense to understand and apply the necessary principles or requirements of life.

I admonish you to remember: it is impossible to establish a righteous government/society that is pleasing to God without the foundation of that government/society being structured upon the Word of God. Needless to say, certainly one would have to know what the laws, statutes, commandments and ordinances of God are, in order to establish a family, community, nation, etc. that is God-like or Godly. This is the clearly understandable motif that has been the guiding light since the Genesis, the command to sanctify or make a difference between the tree of life and the tree of knowledge of good and evil, the clean and the unclean, the Holy and the profane. The use of such terms as life and death, and heaven and hell began with Cain and Abel. This type of terminology was initially used to make or put a difference between the rewards and abodes of God and satan.

For example, "to go to hell" was merely to enter a realm or world where the work for (worship of) God ceases. It implied an end, a cessation of one's maintaining of a high level of God-consciousness. It noted the end of a relationship, not a physical life. Yet in its darkness, it was the equivalent of the grave. The activities in the place called Sheol (hell) were/are in direct opposition to the life and activities in heaven. Those imprisoned and trapped in hell, can be saved only if they institute a new lifestyle or beginning under the rule of God, because His glory covereth the heavens, as the evil of satan covereth hell.

Here seems to be the place for a few salient points concerning life, death and the resurrection of the dead. This exegesis is very critical, and it is pertinent that you refer back to it on many occasions. You must strive to remove the veil concerning life and death that covers and inhibits your mental faculties. You will probably be suprised to know that man's first contact with death was not in the graveyard; nor did life begin in the womb of a woman. Man's life begins in the book of Genesis with the breath of life (intellect of God) being breathed into Adam by God. As a consequence, man is transformed from an exiguous physical structure into a "living soul," or to be more precise, man's soul came alive. This particular creative process was the beginning of life on this planet for our generation.

Also, in the creative process God concerned himself with man's outer appearance, thereby He fashioned him in His image. This process gave meaning and substance to the external body, because he was given by God, the optimum of appearance. Unquestionably this God-like appearance has no equal. In order to execute the will of God, via the external structure or form, God made the hands, legs, eyes, fingernails, etc. Indeed God made the corporeal God-like or God-preferred body from the dust of the earth. The internal set of components (organs) of the body are called the soul. This intricate part of the body makes it the driving force. Only after breath (instructions/sense) was breathed into it, was it invigorated and ready to work for God. This body, soul and spirit entwined is the highest form of existence, called man, and authority to oversee the planet was bestowed upon him. Although God gave Adam dominion over the earth, he was not authorized to exploit it in an evil way, but was to maintain the earth and himself in the God-like, God-preferred manner. In the same general framework of time, man was placed in an environment of conversing trees (attainable knowledge).

"And the Lord God planted a garden eastward in Eden; and there he put the man whom he had formed.

And out of the ground made the Lord God to grow every tree that is pleasant to the sight, and good for food; the tree of life also in the midst of the garden, and the tree of knowledge of good and evil."

Genesis 2:8-9

"And the Lord God commanded the man saying, Of every tree of the garden thou mayest freely eat;

But of the tree of the knowledge of good and evil, thou shalt not *eat of it; for in the day that thou eatest thereof <u>thou shalt surely die.</u>"*

Genesis 2:16-17

"To appoint unto them that mourn in Zion, to give unto them beauty for ashes, the oil of joy for mourning, the garment of praise for the spirit of heaviness; that they might be called trees of righteousness, the planting of the Lord, that he might be glorified."

Isaiah 61:3

"Blessed is the man that walketh not in the counsel of the ungodly, nor standeth in the way of sinners, nor sitteth in the seat of the scornful.

But his delight is in the law of the Lord; and in his law doth he meditate day and night.

And he shall be like a tree planted by the rivers of water, that bringeth forth his fruit in his season; his leaf also shall not wither; and whatsoever he doeth shall prosper."

Psalms 1:1-3

"And it came to pass in the eleventh year, in the third month, in the first day of the month, that the word of the Lord came unto me, saying,

Son of Man, speak unto Pharaoh king of Egypt, and to his multitude, Whom art thou like in thy greatness?

Behold, the Assyrian was a cedar in Lebanon with fair branches, and with a shadowing shroud, and of an high stature; and his top was among the thick boughs.

The waters made him great; the deep set him up on high with her rivers running round about his plants, and sent out her little rivers unto all the trees of the field.

Therefore, his height was exalted above all the trees of the field, and his boughs were multiplied, and his branches became long

163

because of the multitude of waters, when he shot forth.

All the fowls of heaven made their nests in his boughs, and under his branches did all the beasts of the field bring forth their young, and under his shadow dwelt all great nations.

Thus was he fair in his greatness, in the length of his branches; for his root was by great waters.

The cedars in the garden of God could not hide him; the fir trees were not like his boughs, and the chestnut trees were not like his branches, nor any tree in the garden of God was like unto him in his beauty.

I have made him fair by the multitude of his branches, so that all the trees of Eden, that were in the garden of God, envied him."

Ezekiel 31:1-9

These Edenic trees represented those whose attributes were placed in the service of God at the creation of Adam. We could say that they were angels of paradise. After close perusal of the message of Genesis, we ascertain that we are not to visualize these "trees" as having trunks and branches of wood and leaves. We must envisage trees with tongues for talking and knowledge for consumption. This is evident from the wrathful response of God to the strange behavior of Adam and Eve upon His return to the garden. "Who told you that you were naked..." (or with whom have you been conversing)? These trees were to provide all of the required assistance to Adam's intuitive understanding to perfectly fulfill the will of God.

Taking our cue from the greatest director who warned us of the tree of knowledge of good and evil, we shall proceed to give names to some of the trees that were present. We may reasonably conclude that there was an abundance of trees with positive attributes such as: the Tree of Knowledge of Fire, the Tree of Knowledge of Soil, of Air, of Water, of Kindness, of Joy, of Pleasure, of Consumption, of Disposal, of Sharing, of Beauty, of Life's Purpose, etc. Of course, also present was the Tree with the Forked Tongue of Good and Evil.

We bear witness to the unsurpassable loving kindness of God as He gives us access to unimaginable blessings. "Of all the trees of the garden, thou mayest freely eat..." Consider: as much life as you desire, and the same for joy, pleasure, beauty, etc. Deception has taken so much from us and continues to deprive us of all the good things promised by God. You no doubt have noticed the great respect I've shown to my reader by not referring to the image you've always held of the serpent that was "pleasant to the eyes and a tree to be desired to make one wise" being a slithering reptile.

"The fruit of the righteous is a tree of life..."

Proverbs 11:30

It is obvious that the fruit of the unrighteous is a tree of good and evil! Accordingly, man is admonished to consume from (listen to) all the trees as he desires, except he (the tree) that is double-minded, speaking of good and evil. For in the same day that he is influenced by the tree of good and evil, he shall surely die.

This passage marks our first introduction to death. Death was not introduced to us in the dark abandoned cemetery, but in the course of misdirected discussion. Soon thereafter, we find the serpent approaching Eve in an inquiring manner: what are God's instructions unto you concerning the trees? This is still satan's approach until this very day. He innocently asks your opinion of men of God; your reply will determine if he will have access to your mind. Eve responded not according to the instructions that had been given. Her erroneous answer encouraged further dialogue, leading to her deception. In the course of their conversation he revealed himself as the tree of good and evil. But by now his smooth convincing conversation and attractive outward appearance had her hypnotized. (This is very similar to present day humanity [Eve] and the evil world systems.) Consequently, she missed her cue to flee and save her life. Eve allowed herself to become influenced by the tree of knowledge of good and evil. She then convinced Adam to share what she had learned. He, too, did eat, and together they died. "But of the tree of the knowledge of good and evil, thou shall not eat of it; for in the day that thou eatest thereof, thou shall surely die."

165

"Now the serpent was more subtle than any beast of the field which the Lord God had made. And he said unto the woman, Yea, hath God said, Ye shall not eat of every tree of the garden?

And the woman said unto the serpent, We may eat of the fruit of the trees of the garden;

But of the fruit of the tree which is in the midst of the garden, God hath said, Ye shall not eat of it, neither shall ye touch it, lest ye die.

And the serpent said unto the woman, Ye shall not surely die;

For God doth know that in the day ye eat thereof, then your eyes shall be opened, and ye shall be as gods, knowing good and evil.

And when the woman saw that the tree was good for food, and that it was pleasant to the eyes, and a tree to be desired to make one wise, she took of the fruit thereof, and did eat, and gave also unto her husband with her; and he did eat.

And the eyes of them both were opened, and they knew that they were naked; and they sewed fig leaves together and made themselves aprons.

And they heard the voice of the Lord God walking in the garden in the cool of the day: and Adam and his wife hid themselves from the presence of the Lord God amongst the trees of the garden.

And the Lord God called unto Adam, and said unto him, Where art thou?

And he said, I heard thy voice in the garden, and I was afraid, because I was naked; and I hid myself.

And he said, Who told thee that thou wast naked? Hast thou eaten of the tree, whereof I commanded thee that thou shouldest not eat?"

Genesis 3:1-11

At this point death enters for the first time into the realm of the newly-created human family; its reign of fear, pain and destruction has perservered unto the advent of the Kingdom of God. Death has now become so common that it appears quite normal. You are un-mindful of the fact that in the beginning it was forbidden to die. We take note that even the serpent responded with shock and amazement at Eve's statement concerning imminent death being the price to pay for yielding to good and evil influence: "Ye shall not surely die" as if to say "no one dies; you must be mistaken as to what you've been told."

We must understand that death was not desired by God because He is our life if we abide by His creative process. The end of life was not inevitable. It is vividly clear that the decision to die was man's decision, not God's. Our instructions were quite clear... please don't die! Everlasting life is in harmony with the will of God! The inspired author of the book of Genesis now gives us an overview of the events following the first death of Adam and Eve. After consuming the deadly doctrine, it states that the eyes of both were "opened," implying that a spiritual/mental transition had taken place. This is the only logical explanation, since God certainly did not create them blind. The fact is that the new influence of err caused them to see things quite differently. With their new frame of mind the body was affected.

They conceived that they were naked (exposed, vulnerable to the forces of evil) sewed fig leaves together and made themselves aprons. After being cast aside, the body or God-like image is in distress. Adam and Eve die the second death, as they involved themselves in activities which were in contrast and opposition to the instructions (law) given by God.

The next event affects their ears: "And they heard the voice of the Lord God walking in the garden in the cool of the day: and Adam and his wife hid themselves from the presence of the Lord God." Their ears could no longer hear the voice that was good for them; the voice (words) of their God now made them uncomfortable. They ran and have continued running from the presence of the true and living God of Creation. God responded to their foolish acts appropriately: "Who have you been listening to? Who told you that you were naked"?

Man now without mind (spirit) and body (preferred image) has lost his resistance to evil's final, fatal blow. "...Cursed is the ground for thy sake; in sorrow shall thou eat of it all the days of thy life; ...in the sweat of thy face (pain and distress) shall thou eat bread, till thou return unto the ground." The end result, their third death: the death of the soul through cursed consumption from a cursed land.

The cycle is completed. A new awareness has taken control of the biochemistry of the body. Now man measures his time by years in the realm of limited existence, instead of eternity. He is paying a high price for thinking that the grass was greener on the other side of eternal paradise.

Now as we briefly recall events, our introduction to the original form of life was when intellect (God's breath) was breathed into Adam. Similarly we find the first death occurred as a result of losing or changing that mind (sense/intellect) for a double-mind (good and evil). Consider the fact that in the beginning both life and death were directly linked to a form of intellect i.e. sense, or the lack of it.

Living had nothing to do with the weekend party, and death was not initially connected with the cemetery. We also note that after the most significant death of Adam (loss of his God-sense), he was still in the possession of hands, feet, arms, legs and an active physical body. If we recall, these no doubt were the identical physical features of the man Nicodemus who came by night to visit Yeshua. After listening to Nicodemus, Yeshua determined that this scholar, member of the Sanhedrin, teacher and leader, would have to be born again in order to return to the world (Kingdom) of God. In the eyes of the messenger, Nicodemus, like Adam, was dead and in need of a revival of the spirit of God in order that he might see and enter the Kingdom (world) of God. Needless to say, this sounded like a very unrealistic prospect to the well-known, highly-respected Nicodemus. Nicodemus, with all of his titles, pomp and glory, was in fact one of the fallen sons; so were his colleagues.

At this point it should be vividly clear that the death of the body and soul or physical degeneration consummating at being buried in the soil of the graveyard is the final form of a three phase process: (1)

loss of mind (2) loss of soul and body and (3) burial. The final two stages of death do not involve total beings. They have no way to exist of their own accord as part of the creative plan or process. The flesh is neither the determinant of life nor is it the key to sustaining life. All deaths after the first death are merely consequential. If we prevent the cause, the effect (death) must ultimately disappear together with all conscious suffering. In our retrospection, we also are reminded that of the three deaths, one is major and two minor. Nevertheless, they are all noted as deaths.

The first, the most significant and root cause of the others, is the spiritual death: the alienation from God through a process of learning, accepting and being influenced by another thought pattern or mind. This transition leaves the dead with physical eyes that see not, ears in place that hear not and a mind that does not prefer the presence of the God of creation. This change of mentality (mind) leads to the second death. The first by-product and second death, is the death of the body. The outer appearance changes and so do your works or labors as you begin to labor for, toil for, work for, and worship the force that is in opposition to God. You visibly appear dressed in darkness and igno-rance. The light of your countenance is darkened; your oft-verbalized concept of God will not make you Godly. For without a righteous lifestyle and Holy culture, you are trapped in a continuous cycle of decline, depression and destitution which prevents true love, truth, justice, mercy, equity and peaceful harmony. Your new mind caused your human development to be halted and in its place is found eternal damnation and disgrace to you and all who will allow you to influence them. Your arrogance has caused you to forget that the process of human development is an inherent part of a relationship with your maker. When the righteous relationship ends, human development must halt; the unseen law of relativity takes control of your destiny.

The process of human development does not exist in a vacuum; it is perfectly tied into obedience to the God that created you. To think it could be otherwise isn't even logical. An uninterrupted and un-changed involvement with this second death phase leads to the inevitable third death: the death of the soul, the inner organs of man housed by the body. You are now in a state of degeneration - you've lost your mind, so you think any and everything; you've lost your body, so you do any and everything - which subsequently causes you to lose your soul. You are now totally without discipline, and without discipline you lose control of the all-important order of your life.

"Wisdom is glorious, and never fadeth away: yea, she is easily seen of them that love her, and found of such as seek her."

"For the very true beginning of her is the desire of discipline; and the care of discipline is love;

And love is the keeping of her laws; and the giving heed unto her laws is the assurance of incorruption; And incorruption maketh us near unto God: Therefore the desire of wisdom bringeth to a kingdom."

Wisdom of Solomon 6:12, 17-20 (Apocrypha)

Whenever an organization or community stresses discipline, they are immediately labelled a "cult," which carries with it a multiplicity of negative connotations. This is a tactic employed effectively by the media - agents of the satanic system - to destroy the credibility of that organization or community. With the simple use of a term it severs access to the public at large, denying the opportunity for intelligent consideration of the substance of the message. Do not be afraid nor discouraged, for this is the essence of spiritual warfare. Nevertheless, discipline holds the vital key to our reunification with our God.

Over the years I've noticed that the highest forms of the performing arts are referred to as "disciplines." The highest forms of the martial arts are also called "disciplines." Considering these two aspects together with every aspect of professional achievement, wherein the key element is discipline, it should not take much mental effort to conclude that the highest form of life is/was and shall always be a disciplined life.

The law was not given as a guide to daily ritualism; it was given as a reminder of the need for discipline in our lives. Without discipline, the soul cannot enter the higher spiritual realm called "Heaven," or life under the dominion of God. The adversary of God prefers an undisciplined society, which keeps the human family in a realm called "hell," or life (death) under the dominance of the satanic spirit. This force of evil has caused unimaginable suffering to befall the family of nations from sense-preventable disease and destruction. The Euro-gentile emphasis on creed instead of conduct and discipline in man's quest for God allowed the subtle inclusion of his sacrosanct paganism. He brought his old pagan holidays, his vain customs and his structured systems of false worship into his "new religion" unnoticed, consolidating his firm grip on the old as well as the new. To his old faithful constituents and the now deceived world at large, these pagan practices were/are seen as harmless fabrications to those who "just believe." Your life and environment are now so dominated by lies until you are rendered incapable of dealing honestly with yourself or others.

Immediately after your resurrection, (I fervently pray that you experience one), you must move expediently to sanctify yourselves through faith in the God of Israel and Holiness as demonstrated through the development of a conduct that finds pleasure in the eyes of God. Though you may fall short from time to time, it is yet a vast difference in the eyes of God between he that trains diligently, participates and falls short in a race and he that does not train nor participate. He loses by forfeit. One knocked on the door trying to enter; the other never knocked at all. He that has ears to hear, let him hear.

Undisciplined, liberal democracy is as deadly as an overdose of D.D.T. or other carcinogenic substances. It creates a social sphere below what was once considered ordinary life. Since you are without proper mental faculties, certainly you do not realize that it is the iniquity and ill-dealing of liberal democracy that has laid waste the whole earth. Surely wickedness has altered your understanding, and beguiled your soul to the extent that things that are honest and true are obscured unto you. Remember, everything is negatively affected by disorder. We should therefore see discipline as merely taking control of our lives. My wholehearted feeling is that once we take firm control of our lives, we will progressively find ourselves in control of life itself. Your soul (inner organisms) now has little chance of survival with your mind and body working against it. Gradually, the cardiovascular, digestive, immune and other systems are overwhelmed and destroyed by disorder; the organs become broken down and plagued by strange viruses, diseases, ailments, infirmities and malfunction. All of this is a result of you now being engulfed in sin.

The wages of sin is the death of your soul, culminating with your being "laid to rest" in your tomb. Your poor soul suffers greatly under the burden of ignorance as you sniff membrane-destroying cocaine into your nostrils, inhale tobacco smoke in your lungs and sip alcohol into your mouth. You dine on an endless variety of animal carcasses, small rats (a Chinese delicacy) from the cellar and larger rats (opossum) from the forest, unborn calves, chicken embryos, crabs, lobsters, dogs, hogs and frogs. Of course you start your day with a glass full of a cow's milk that was naturally created to nourish her calf. Absolutely udder foolishness! What kind of mind would cause a body to put such things into the soul of a human? Certainly not a smart one. You've made so much progress in your war against life, and because of your present demented state, you do not realize that you've succeeded in destroying your own. To the victor goes the spoils; you are a master of hell and all of your inhabitants are dead.

The soul, properly cared for, is the most perfect healing mechanism ever created. With proper care and use within the cycles and seasons of God, it will dispose of all of its waste, both solids and liquids. Waste elimination is of supreme importance. Why is it so seldom mentioned or stressed by the recognized medical establishment in contemporary society? The deluded human family is much more proficient at eliminating waste from their homes than from their bodies. They are cognizant of the negative effects of parasites that appear when waste is left in the garbage pail at home, but are inept at understanding what is taking place in the colon when feces aren't properly eliminated. People are being literally poisoned daily by their own waste - another example of man being his own worst enemy.

Man today, lacking the sense and reason motivated by God and life, responds to such reasoning with a logic that is inappropriate, often to an absurd degree. From the minds of the ancients, we deduce that matter (the soul) is both solid and liquid, collectively creating a whole.

As the liquid is in a constant state of change and transformation, flow and movement, it is the former of the solids or the life of the solids. The solids then, are still of the liquids. These substances are controlled by a spirit. If the soul's spirit is not properly oriented, it will negatively affect the flow and removal of the liquid, and thus the formation and excretion of solids. We can still conclude that they are all one.

We determine that everlasting was/is continuous God-mind controlled change. When the unity of thought which equals life is broken, man removes himself from the realm of the everlasting and enters a cycle of decadence and death. Thus the human soul (existence) is a complex web of organs that are relative to a unified whole.

The soul has a defense system second to none, which will mobilize itself instantly, secreting antibodies which will attack and destroy any virus as well as repair all injured tissues and organs. The soul can replace old blood with new every 90 days, create new cells every 11 months and even bone structure every two years. We cannot maintain something so precious with inferior materials (junk food). What you put into it today will determine what it will withstand tomorrow. Remember, with loving God-care, it was originally created to function forever. Instead, it has been attacked and beaten with the diligence and ferociousness of an insane enemy, whose purpose was to destroy totally this incomparable creation of God. The soul, beaten into submission, can no longer offer much resistance to disease, whereby it no longer functions within the life cycle of God, but in the death cycle of its adversary. If it could be totalled, the moans and groans which have been heard and the pain which has been felt by the human body during the last two hundred years of rule of the modern Euro-American would greatly surpass all the moans, groans and pain of the preceding five thousand, eight hundred years combined. There has never been a time in history when we could so confidantly state that everyone is sick, suffering or dismembered (35 million operations are performed yearly in America alone). Before the coming of the Euro-gentile dominion, man and the creation had never suffered so much and so regularly: the axe is taken to the trees, the gun to the birds and the scalpel to man.

Let us be truthful with ourselves: only truth, justice, mercy, love of

God and righteousness will transform this so-called progressive society, not technological advancement and scientific research.

In concluding this particular exegesis of the creation and fall into oblivion as recorded in the book of Genesis, we have explained to you the process as it relates to the three deaths: the spirit (the mind), the body (the external appearance and works), and the soul (the preparation for the graveyard). This prophetic pattern also gives our pretext for concluding that if there were three deaths, of a necessity there will be three resurrections in the redemptive plan. Let us first consider the definition of "resurrection"

English language: *a resurgence (a rising again into life, activity, or prominence); revival (resuscitate, to stir up, to put into motion, to revive from apparent death or from unconsciousness, to revitalize); a spiritualization of thought, the rising again to life (the chance to live) of all the human dead before the final judgment.*

Hebrew language: *an awakening to a new life, a revival of the Holy Spirit (the breath of life of Genesis, the God-mind.)*

"The resurrection is really the day of triumph for the Word of God; the day when God's word will suddenly come alive and instill in men the desire to live again under the simple rulership of God. It will come again through a body of men who will invoke the presence of God on earth and give the people a plan of redemption and show them in truth and through works the way back to God. The people in turn would, as a reward from God for obedience, be given the keys to everlasting life outside the realms and literal bounds of society (hell on earth). We will experience paradise - a world without end, a world of the original creation, a world wherein men live together as brethren without fear. For us, as it is written, hearing is the first means of salvation. You must hear the trumpet: the trumpet is the Word of God. The Word will come forth first. First was the Word and the Word was God. The Word will be spoken, written and sung. The Word will have a message - a message of deliverance from hell. You are in hell now. You must be delivered."

God the Black Man and Truth
by Ben Ammi, Communicators Press.

THE GENESIS RESURRECTION

In contemporary history, the Bible consists of the Old and New Testaments. However, in every exegesis on a Biblical subject it is pertinent to begin study in the Old Testament. We easily discover that all subjects based on truth throughout the Bible have their base and roots - directly or indirectly - in the Old Testament. One of the principal reasons for much of the confusion and/or misunderstanding concerning the things written about Yeshua is that the teachers and lay individuals have disassociated themselves from the earlier writings in the Hebrew canon. Euro-American theological institutions do not seriously encourage the focused study of the ancient revelations of Moses and the inspired prophets. They tenaciously hold fast to a false belief that the coming of Yeshua has somehow fulfilled these eternal and sacred writings. However, they contain the highest form of ethical intructions (law) and an uncannnily accurate forecast of events (prophecy) that continue to maintain their relevance up to our day.

Those in control of the power to define gave us a New Testament, and subtly transposed its authority to supersede that of the ancient writings of the Old Testament. Now when the Bible is mentioned, the layman thinks of Matthew, Mark, Luke, etc. The fact is there is no

175

Bible void of the Old Testament. The Biblical interpolaters formulated the term "New Testament" which subsequently created the need for an "Old Testament." After thoroughly separating the soul from the body (oldest from new), religious leaders tell you that the Old Testament has fulfilled its purpose. Well, if that be the case, then your body can exist without the head, or vice-versa.

The truth of the matter is that the authentic writings in the New Testament exist only if they are rooted in the Old Testament (Hebrew canon) - the inspired writings of the prophets and messengers of God. No one can understand the Messianic message of Yeshua without a very thorough review and study of the ancient Hebraic writings. A teacher or novice that opens a 200 page book and begins to read on page 101 feeling that he thoroughly understands it is being remiss to himself and whomever he has to convey the full substance of the book.

Lest I make the same mistake, I will extract from the first book of the Bible (Genesis) in my brief dissertation on the resurrection. I am very cognizant of the fact that in the beginning, man was given "intuitive understanding," a definitive quality or trait of the active God-mind. This was a natural form of intellect that was inherent in man. In the beginning, the Omnipotent God endowed man with an instinctive knowledge, an inborn tendency to act or respond in a particular way relative to the source of his creation - the land. This active principle of the God-mind allowed man to properly discern how to preserve the creations of God and how to wisely use the revelations of knowledge about God's creation. Therefore, man in his "right mind" possesses instinctive understanding as to why he should not pollute the water he must drink, the air he must breathe and the food he must eat. Thus by the active principle of the God-mind, man was able to maintain the ecological order and harmony of the creations and insure his existence within that order.

The generations after the fall brought about many changes in this understanding. Man was in a constant state of mental and physical degeneracy. Because such a condition existed, his ability to comprehend truth waned, and his moral standards decreased. Consequently, many nations began formulating laws and statutes that they interpreted and taught according to the realities that surrounded them. We must unanimously conclude and agree that, as with any people in a state of decadence, their ability to understand is affected. The original intent of Genesis was losing its effectiveness as the understanding of the nations of old slowly ebbed away. With each passing generation, man's perception and natural inherent ability to grasp what is right failed him. He understood less and less until he arrived at his lowest point, a time when studying the contents of the ancient Hebraic Bible was even discouraged. The Children of Israel were chosen to keep a semblance of the former order and understanding in the midst of the nations. Together with the prophets and wise men of other nations, they periodically pleaded in God's name to the fallen human family. Bear in mind, that prophets weren't always with us nor was there need for them, and in the coming age, they will again disappear from the scene. As a matter of fact, it will be forbidden to prophecy. Nevertheless, all of the masters of today are being moved by the spirit of the God of creation to herald the advent of a new beginning, a new genesis, and the dire necessity for the same.

Could we possibly acknowledge the magnitude of far-reaching changes in the understanding and subsequent interpretations of the message of Genesis without using the same measuring rod concerning the resurrection? Certainly not. What was referred to as the resurrection during the times of the ancients is certainly not what is being alluded to as the resurrection in our generation.

There is no parallel between the state of deviancy of contemporary society and the sins of our fathers only a generation ago. If you recall, the trends defined as normal during your childhood and those of the present day are worlds apart. What qualified one as a nice little boy or girl during my childhood and what is considered socially acceptable today for nice children are worlds apart. Not so long ago young men had a wide selection of virgin daughters to choose from to become their wives. Today, hardly a woman arrives to adulthood as a virgin. I recall when losing virginity before marriage was the exception. Today it has been redefined as a normal part of growing up. To come home with a baby was considered a socially punishable crime. Men were not anxious for a relationship with a careless, or as we once said, a "loose" woman, or vice versa.

This was all a part of an inborn social attitude to assist in the prevention of illicit behavior. Now you sit and watch your young daughters lose their chastity even before they reach their teens. Your advice: be certain to require the use of a condom. I remember if a condom was seen discarded on the streets we would all be embarrassed. My, how things have changed... for the worst! The devil, who was once an evil outcast, has now found widespread acceptance, disguised as an angel of light pushing an innocent "alternative lifestyle."

The unsuspecting public is being groomed to accept homosexuality also as a natural alternative lifestyle. This, of course, will have the expected results of increasing acts of perversion. In their inaugural years in school, children will be irreparably confused as to what are normal sexual roles for men and women. They'll soon think that the God-sanctioned family model is merely one of a number of options. Two married women are just as natural as man and woman. I'm certain that the evil that haunts us in the streets and in our homes daily was previously encouraged in some subtle fashion or form. Today's television programs like "The Oprah Winfrey Show" are applauded for bringing viewers issues of lesbian mothers or homosexual fathers. "Join us tomorrow for gay transvestites: people who changed their sex to have sex with the same sex." We allow this type of ridiculousness in our homes without a whimper of protest! This ungodly behavior has led to the decline and dissolution of the entire Euro-gentile society, and all who have patterned themselves after them.

It now appears that whoever is in control of the power to define has redefined evil to the point where it and the people are very comfortable roommates. Social behavior that not so long ago was considered deviant is becoming more and more acceptable. Someone seems to be striving to accustom us to a lifestyle that will perpetuate our alienation from God. Perverted activities that should cause great alarm in your midst go unnoticed as if your minds are in a type of stupor. That is to say, once upon a time it was necessary for evil to sneak into your lives. But now it has been redefined and subsequently walks straight through the front door. Regretfully, you have fallen victim to your own permissiveness and lack of understanding.

178

In order to be saved from this eternal destruction, man must now learn to think and act anew. Today, we must reinterpret the inspired writings of the prophets in order to guide the human family back to the old paths. Only by reawakening God in your lives can we help those of you who are seeking resurrection and redemption in these final days of the rule and dominion of European civilization.

As we profoundly and truthfully study the contents of the message of the creation, our first revelation concerning the resurrection is that it did not exist. We draw this important conclusion because there was no death; life was eternal. There was no doctrine of the resurrection; it was not needed and was not a part of the understanding of the earlier human family. It was formulated much later, probably thousands of years after the fall of Adam. We accept, consequently, that the original promise of eternal life and the final reward of everlasting life nullifies the need for such a philosophy. The concept of a resurrection can only hold a temporary significance because it neither existed in the beginning nor has it a prophetic permanency. The need for a doctrine of resurrection could only have arisen after the advent of death. Since the original death was spiritual - a loss or change of mind and direction which alienates us from God - then the original resurrection had to be a return to a/the former God consciousness.

Again it is written in Genesis that Adam and Eve's eyes were "opened" after they had been influenced by the tree of knowledge of good and evil. This statement is very important because we draw from it the fact that they had eyes. However, after their eyes were opened, it appears their natural and spiritual vision was darkened. This latter opening of their eyes is tied directly to a state of unconsciousness, or death; in the former pristine state their eyes could neither see evil nor discern good and evil simultaneously.

As we take further note of life spans in the early centuries, we have accounts of men living hundreds of years; the transition was not spontaneous, but took place gradually. Remember: "...for in the day that thou eatest thereof thou shalt surely die (enter into the cycles and process of death)." Therefore, for hundreds and probably thousands of years, the degeneration of the soul was not a major factor in the formulation of thought patterns of the human family. However, evil

179

and decadence had an immediate devastating effect on their lives and thinking.

This fact allows us to authoritatively conclude that all discussion of resurrection in the formative years only referred to the return of the God-mind - a re-opening of the eyes of the dead to the vision of God. They were not talking of a calling out of cemeteries, because for all practical purposes they did not exist in the manner known today. They came into existence in the following generations. This being the only death familiar to them predicated the only resurrection sought after: a halting of spiritual and mental decadence and a re-opening their eyes to God's instructions and the original natural life-sustaining laws of the planet. All other doctrine of the resurrection was formulated as both body and soul continued on an uninterrupted path of damnation and decadence.

Man was soon faced with more realities of his sordid state of existence on this planet. Other forms of death advented along with shorter life (death) cycles without God. This created the need for the formulation of newer and broader theological and psychological resurrection treatises that would be more suitable to generations more in tune with death of the soul. The spirit of error sought to make the ever increasing frequency of this final death the principal plague of contemporary man during his sojourn on this sacred planet of ours - more palatable to the masses.

In further considering man's fall into oblivion, we see that though his eyes are opened, he stumbles as a blind man at noonday. Considering what has befallen man's eyes shines a great light upon the numerous Biblical verses and prophecies referring to the Children of Israel (the Sons and Daughters of Light) as being "blind." A principal Messianic promise is that the Anointed of God would cause the blind to see and heal the sick (soul). These Biblical references are no doubt referring to the re-opening of the eyes that were closed in the book of Genesis. This is not to negate the physical miracles performed from time to time by the men and/or messengers of God, but is in reference to the broader aspects of the removal of the spiritual blindness which afflicts our people. In re-opening their eyes, the Anointed would restore the vision of God, for the family of nations now have eyes that see not, ears that hear not and a mind that is alienated from God. It should at this time be evident that the highest form of unadulterated and undiluted expectations concerning the resurrection is the original manner in which men were reborn, prior to the need for such a doctrine. This form is the spiritual/mental resurrection, the original form of the resurrection found in Genesis.

Let us also consider the close parallel between those mentally/ spiritually dead and the corpses of the cemetery. In the message of Ezekiel, we find a very vivid illustration of how the God of Israel allegorically views those that have turned aside to the pursuit of falsehood:

"The hand of the Lord was upon me, and carried me out in the spirit of the Lord, and set me down in the midst of the valley which was full of bones,

And caused me to pass by them round about; and, behold, there were very many in the open valley; and, lo, they were very dry. And he said unto me, Son of man, can these bones live? And I answered, O Lord God, thou knowest.

Again he said unto me, Prophesy upon these bones: and say unto them, O ye dry bones, hear the word of the Lord.

Thus saith the Lord God unto these bones, Behold, I will cause breath to enter into you, and ye shall live.

And I will lay sinews upon you, and will bring up flesh upon you, and cover you with skin, and put breath in you, and ye shall live; and ye shall know that I am the Lord.

So I prophesied as I was commanded. And as I prophesied, there was a noise and, behold, a shaking, and the bones came together, bone to his bone.

And when I beheld, lo, the sinews and the flesh came up upon them, and the skin covered them above, but there was no breath in them.

Then said he unto me, Prophesy unto the wind, prophesy, son of man, and say to the wind, Thus saith the Lord God: Come from the four winds, O breath, and breathe upon these slain, that they may live.

So I prophesied as he commanded me, and the breath came into them, and they lived, and stood up upon their feet, an exceedingly great army.

Then he said unto me, Son of man, these bones are the whole house of Israel; behold, they say, Our bones are dried, and our hope is lost; we are cut off for our parts.

Therefore, prophesy and say unto them, Thus saith the Lord God: Behold, O my people, I will open your graves, and cause you to come up out of your graves, and bring you into the land of Israel.

And ye shall know that I am the Lord, when I have opened your graves, O my people, and brought you up out of your graves,

And shall put my Spirit in you, and ye shall live, and I shall place you in your own land; then shall ye know that I, the Lord, have spoken it, and performed it, saith the Lord."

Ezekiel 37:1-14

Here in Ezekiel, we see the close correlation between the spiritual and physical dead. As a matter of fact, the principal point clarified is that amongst the mentally and mortally dead in the eyes of Ezekiel, there is no difference whatsoever. Therefore, as you persist in the study of the Bible, be very circumspect in drawing conclusions concerning a resurrection of the corporeal dead, for it is more likely alluding to the resurrection of a dead mind/spirit. Here again, resurrection is projected in the original form of the Genesis.

At this point it is necessary to remind you that in a world sustained by deception, an excessive amount of truth is very hard to cope with. Truth is the lethal weapon to be used against a lie. We call to mind the words of Ezekiel, the inspired prophet of God, as well as many other prophetic references that testify to the state of darkness that is prevalent over the earth and its inhabitants. They give us a clear perspective of the evident nexus between the literal and allegorical graveyards described, as a place of extreme darkness.

Another explicit illustration is rendered by Isaiah the prophet:

"Arise, shine; for thy light is come, and the glory of the Lord is risen upon thee.

For, behold, the darkness shall cover the earth, and gross darkness the peoples, but the Lord shall arise upon thee, and his glory shall be seen upon thee.

And the nations shall come to thy light, and kings to the brightness of thy rising."

Isaiah 60:1-3

"Arise, shine," is a clear command to move from darkness into light. Your/this resurrection is synonymous with the return of the glory of God, a distinct difference between your former state of death wherein you gave the glory unto satan. "For, behold the darkness (spiritual ignorance and blindness) covers the earth, and gross darkness (glaring spiritual ignorance and blindness) the people." This is the same condition that was seen by Ezekiel. The nations without God have become a veritable hell on earth, and the burial place for the fallen Sons of God that have become ensnared in a mental bondage.

To be defined as dead in the spiritual context means: having no knowledge of God (double-minded = zero where God is concerned); being in a helpless predicament, wherein one no longer hears, sees, discerns or moves. The African American community today is lying helpless in its grave, covered with the dirt of false gods, false doctrines, false worship, false history, envy, strife, disunity, disrespect, hate of one another and a diet fit for the dead.

When the light of God comes into this world, it is hated because it reveals the evils that have been hidden in darkness. This world only loves its own. It loves you because you are of the same mind. If you were not children of darkness born of adulterated doctrine, it would not love you. In contrast, if you were not one and the same with this world, you could not love it. Your preference is darkness; you fear to come into the light because your evil deeds would be exposed.

The greatest obstacle to an individual being born again is the embarrassment that he has to face concerning his own past: having to acknowledge before family and friends, superiors and subordinates that he has been wrong. This is definitely the quandary that confronted Nicodemus, the acknowledged scholar and honorable member of the highest legal body in Yeshua's day. He was undoubtedly shaken at the discovery that he was a dead man, having to seek a new birth that he may enter the world of God. My people, too, are trapped in the shackles of titles and positions of honor. Without the "God-mind," they cannot understand life's purpose nor fulfill their mission in life. Because of this void in their understanding, their lives have plummeted to a low level of guesswork forever vacillating between good and evil. They are lost and flummoxed in utter darkness.

These words that I speak unto you must electrify you, causing change and movement, causing you to spring up and into action on behalf of God. Can the flesh resurrect the mind, or does the mind resurrect the flesh? Yeshua said "It is the spirit that giveth life; the flesh profits nothing. The words I speak unto you (the sense I give you) they are spirit and they are life." Actually there are very few places in the ancient Hebrew Bible where there is even a mention of a possible resurrection. This subject was not addressed in even one central theme in the inspired writings of Moses and the prophets. Where it is mentioned, I am certain that the author was referring to the resurrection from the fallen (dead) state of Genesis. Yet when you initially read these particular verses, it could be translated either way as I have mentioned previously.

Allow me to include here a few significant points from the recently published writings of the ancient Qumran Hebrew community. Among the most intriguing of the newly-released Dead Sea Scrolls is a fragment that was originally named "On Resurrection." The official editors have now changed the name of this text to "Messianic Apocalypse." It may be easier just to call it "4Q521" (i.e. Document 521 from Qumran Cave 4). After close perusal, I've concluded that it is a very important text, for in the clearest possible language, it describes the resurrection of the dead expected to occur during the Messianic Age. They wrote: "He will heal the sick, resurrect the dead..." I, too, can assure you that there must be a resurrection during this, the Kingdom Age. The only difference is the area of concentration. They, except in error, could not have been implying a resurrection of the flesh, as we are guided by the interpolators to think primarily because that isn't life.

We recall in the aforementioned prophecy of Ezekiel, that even after receiving sinews, flesh and skin, they still had no life until the breath (mind/spirit) was given unto them. The flesh was of no living significance without the mind, which is the determining factor if there is life in existence. If that be the case, then an actual physical resurrection is impossible, the word resurrection itself holding the key. If it is to be a resurrection, there has to be a return of life. This form of resurrection supersedes a corporeal restoration. Because of the fact that the physical body alone cannot determine life, the "resurrected" individual would still be considered dead; that is to say, not resurrected. No matter how many times we replay the scene, the visible return of his flesh would not return life unto him. Only upon receiving a newly-resurrected mind, could anyone have received absolute life. This new mind (spirit/intellect/thought pattern) will manifest a new body.

The coming of the Messiah is definitely the time for the restoration of life unto the dead, the healing of the sick and the opening of the eyes of the blind. But it is also a time of great spiritual warfare. It was satan that had the control of the power to define, subsequently it was he who defined life, death and the resurrection. It was he who directed our attention to the sky, the graveyard, and a resurrection of inanimate flesh. This was because he did not want you to know that you were already dead! He has been so busy promoting "the good life" in his abode in order to divert my/your attention from the death, blindness and darkness that is prevalent in his world. He daily promulgates his adverse doctrine that exalts the good life of his kingdom (hell). Satan now has to face disgrace before the resurrected Sons of God who will not be seduced by the glitter and glamour of his trappings. Remember, satan has deceived the whole world. He had to convince the dead that they were alive so they would not seek life. I admonish all to remember that just to possess a body, no matter how talented, is not sufficient; a body without God-sense does not equate life.

Possibly as you turn the pages of this book, you are beginning to realize more and more with every page and every word, that during your entire sojourn upon this planet earth you've never experienced life. Except that you hear these words, you never will. Perhaps now it is clearer to you as to why they stoned the prophets and killed the former standard bearers of truth. Conceivably, if I were in close proximity, you'd consider doing the same to me for shining this light into your million dollar casket.

This historical epoch is called the Messianic Era, or Judgment Day. What is Judgment Day? Judgment Day is when the Anointed of God lifts up His/their voice from Jerusalem and through the grace of God, gives the earth's inhabitants a final chance to live. It is when the wisdom of God will judge the wisdom of satan, the knowledge of God shall reveal truth to correct ancient misconceptions, and the understanding of God shall make the way so simple until even a fool could not error. It is a time of great hope for the poor. A time to renew their strength (give them purpose). It is the dawn of a New Age. In effect, it is a new creation.

As we develop a positive and effective course of action, we shall begin with some significant scriptural references from Isaiah and Matthew.

> *"Go through, go through the gates; prepare ye the way of the people; cast up, cast up the highway; gather out the stones; lift up a standard for the peoples."*

Isaiah 62:10

> *"And this gospel of the kingdom shall be preached in all the world for a witness unto all nations; and then shall the end come."*

Matthew 24:14

> *"The word that Isaiah, the son of Amoz, saw concerning Judah and Jerusalem.*
>
> *And it shall come to pass in the last days, that the mountain of the Lord's house shall be established in the top of the mountains, and shall be exalted above the hills; and all nations shall flow unto it.*

And many people shall go and say, Come ye, and let us go up to
the mountain of the Lord, to the house of the God of Jacob; and
he will teach us of his ways, and we will walk in his paths; for out
of Zion shall go forth the law, and the word of the Lord from
Jerusalem."

Isaiah 2:1-3

The three aforementioned scriptural references are all relating to the same framework of time: the last days of Euro-gentile dominion. I will draw my explanation from the instructions of Isaiah, "to lift up (set) a standard for the people." In most instances when relating to the Bible, the masses that do read it are usually lost in the "just grace," "just faith" and "just believe" preachments and interpretations of Paul. This leaves them with a very superficial understanding to say the least. If I were to inquire as to what is expected during the resurrection of Judgment Day, the answers would no doubt be far, far away from describing the events that are actually taking place. Yeshua said "And except those days (these days) should be shortened, there should no flesh be saved (left alive)." (Matthew 24:22) Thus, the ultimate objective of satan is to destroy all flesh from off the face of this planet. His ultimate objective is that no one escapes. The Messianic challenge is to shorten his time (dominion/rule) that he not succeed.

Now consider, there could be no resurrection unless the resurrected are set in a Godly established order or governed by a standard that will guide and protect them. The prophet has instructed the Saints of the Kingdom to set the standard. What standard? The standard for the New World, the Kingdom of God, the Resurrection. That is defined to mean there has to be a known and stable measuring rod, not liberal democratic, secular confusion.

There are more than ten thousand different religions in the world as of this writing, with no end in sight. There are two thousand in America alone. There aren't enough years in a man's current lifetime to try them all, and it is for that reason that we have been instructed to set a standard for the nations. For what other reason has God established His Kingdom other than for it to be used as the measuring rod? There has to be a new standard acceptable unto God; a standard of worship; a standard of brotherhood, sisterhood, true love of God.

187

Womanhood, manhood, childhood, consumption, acceptable culture and true wealth. The great spiritual significance of the return of the Sons and Daughters of God (the Children of Israel) and the subsequent establishing of the Kingdom of God, is that it signalled the end of evil Euro-gentile standards ruling over God's creation and people.

The resurrected word of God is the major destabilizer, bringing all evil standards into judgment. Those that come now unto God must believe that He exists and dedicate their lives after their new birth unto Him. Not many will have the vision to recognize the choice of a lifetime that is before us. Then there are those who may well recognize this truth, but will regretfully choose darkness instead of light.

It will not just be the House of Israel that will set these standards. As it is written in the book of Isaiah, the prophet, many shall come up to be taught, for the law and instructions shall go forth from the New World Spiritual Center at the New Jerusalem. Isaiah has admonished on two occasions the arduous task of sorting through the many different perspectives and persuasions: "Remove the stones (obstacles to true progress)" and "many shall be rebuked (made to change)." Nevertheless, many of those journeying up to Jerusalem will also contribute their greatness in the continuous formulation of new world standards. The Kingdom of God has surely come. Yeshua said the doctrine of this Kingdom would be disseminated to all the nations of the planet, giving them their final chance. It would be the choice of a lifetime: to live forever in a heaven on earth or to die in hopes of going to a heaven that existed only in the deceptive doctrine of Euro-gentile theology.

> *"I call heaven and earth to record this day against you, that I have set before you life and death, blessing and cursing; therefore, choose life, that both thou and thy seed may live,*
>
> *That thou mayest love the Lord thy God, and that thou mayest obey his voice, and that thou mayest cleave unto him; for he is thy life, and the length of thy days; that thou mayest dwell in the land which the Lord swore unto thy fathers, to Abraham, to Isaac, and to Jacob, to give them."*

Deuteronomy 30:19-20

BIBLIOGRAPHY

1. <u>Modern Education: One Size Fits All</u>, Bergin & Garvey Publishers, Inc. c/o Greenwood Publishing Group.

2. "Is Depo Provera Safe?" <u>MS Magazine</u>, January/February 1993, p. 72.

3. John Lovell, Jr., <u>Black Song: The Forge and the Flame</u> (New York: Paragon House Publishers, 1986).

4. Deepak Chopra, M.D., <u>Ageless Body Timeless Mind</u> (New York: Harmony Books, 1993)

5. Daniel Ben Gabriel, <u>The Alternative (A New Perspective on History, Jesus and the Law)</u>.

6. Sir John Hawkins, <u>Declaration of the Troublesome Voyage of Sir John Hawkins to Guinea and the Indies</u>, (New York: Da Capo Press, Inc. (a subsidiary of Plenum Publishing, 1973).

7. Lerone Bennett, Jr., <u>Before the Mayflower: A History of the Negro in America</u>, (Chicago: Johnson Publishing Co.).

8. Walter S. Ross, "At Last, An Anti-Cancer Diet", <u>Readers Digest</u>, February 1983, p. 78.

9. Dianne Joy Goodman and Ted L. Howard, "Communicator, Newsletter of the Organic Crop Improvement Association (International) Inc. , January 1993.

10. "Sex and Booze Turn Hill into a School for Scandal," The Washington Times, March 2, 1989.

11. "Brothers Loving Brothers," an excerpt from the Spectrum, AIDS Education to the Black Community, Washington, D.C.

12. "The Devil's Disciple, The Pitiless Predator" and "More Unsettling News On the Rape Epidemic" Time, January 11, 1993 and May 4, 1992.

13. "The Fatal Triangle: Crack and Syphilis Spread AIDS Among the Poor: Sexual Binges" and "Scouting's Sex Abuse Trial Leads to 50 States", The New York Times, August 20, 1989.

14. "Unsettling Report on an Epidemic of Rape," Time, May 4, 1992.

15. "Child Prostitution Spreads, Partly Because of AIDS Fears" and "Discovery of Heads Points to US Black Market in Body Parts", International Herald Tribune, April 10-11, 1993.

16. "Terror Stalks the Nations Capital, Gunman Takes Aim At Anyone" and "Trading Places, World's First. . . " USA Today, April 13, 1993.

17. Theodore D. Walker, Empower the People (New York: Orbis Books).

18. "Waiter, There's A Rat in My Soup, And It's Delicious!", Wall Street Journal, May 31, 1991.

19. "(Abortion) Murdered for Cosmetics," The Muslim Journal.

20. "The Straight Dope: Gerbil Stuffing?," The Chicago Reader.

21. "It's a Boy, Says Male Mother-to-Be," The Royal Gazette.

22. "Scouting's Sex Abuse Trial Leads to 50 States" The Washington Times, May 20, 1991.

Communicators Press

To order other books by Ben Ammi complete the order blank below and give the others to a friend or family member that they may further their understanding about God, His People and His Plan.

For more information or wholesale requests, write:

**Communicators Press, P.O. Box 26063
Washington, D.C. 20001**

Name _____

Address_____

City, State, Zip Code_____

Everlasting Life

Please enclose $17.00 plus $3.50 shipping & handling and mail to:

**Communicators Press
P.O. Box 26063, Washington, D.C. 20001**

Name _____

Address_____

City, State, Zip Code_____

Everlasting Life

Please enclose $17.00 plus $3.50 shipping & handling and mail to:

**Communicators Press
P.O. Box 26063, Washington, D.C. 20001**

Name _____

Address_____

City, State, Zip Code_____

Everlasting Life

Please enclose $17.00 plus $3.50 shipping & handling and mail to:

**Communicators Press
P.O. Box 26063, Washington, D.C. 20001**

Communicators Press

To order other books by Ben Ammi complete the order blank below and give the others to a friend or family member that they may further their understanding about God, His People and His Plan.

For more information or wholesale requests, write:

Communicators Press, P.O. Box 26063
Washington, D.C. 20001

Name _____

Address_____

City, State, Zip Code_____

The Messiah and the End of This World

Please enclose $17.00 plus $3.50 shipping & handling and mail to:

Communicators Press
P.O. Box 26063, Washington, D.C. 20001

Name _____

Address_____

City, State, Zip Code_____

The Messiah and the End of This World

Please enclose $17.00 plus $3.50 shipping & handling and mail to:

Communicators Press
P.O. Box 26063, Washington, D.C. 20001

Name _____

Address_____

City, State, Zip Code_____

The Messiah and the End of This World

Please enclose $17.00 plus $3.50 shipping & handling and mail to:

Communicators Press
P.O. Box 26063, Washington, D.C. 20001

Communicators Press

To order other books by Ben Ammi complete the order blank below and give the others to a friend or family member that they may further their understanding about God, His People and His Plan.

For more information or wholesale requests, write:

**Communicators Press, P.O. Box 26063
Washington, D.C. 20001**

Name _____

Address_____

City, State, Zip Code_____

God and The Law of Relativity

Please enclose $15.00 plus $3.50 shipping & handling and mail to:

**Communicators Press
P.O. Box 26063, Washington, D.C. 20001**

Name _____

Address_____

City, State, Zip Code_____

God and The Law of Relativity

Please enclose $15.00 plus $3.50 shipping & handling and mail to:

**Communicators Press
P.O. Box 26063, Washington, D.C. 20001**

Name _____

Address_____

City, State, Zip Code_____

God and The Law of Relativity

Please enclose $15.00 plus $3.50 shipping & handling and mail to:

**Communicators Press
P.O. Box 26063, Washington, D.C. 20001**

Communicators Press

To order other books by Ben Ammi complete the order blank below and give the others to a friend or family member that they may further their understanding about God, His People and His Plan.

For more information or wholesale requests, write:

Communicators Press, P.O. Box 26063
Washington, D.C. 20001

Name _____

Address_____

City, State, Zip Code_____

God the Black Man and Truth

Please enclose $15.00 plus $3.50 shipping & handling and mail to:

Communicators Press
P.O. Box 26063, Washington, D.C. 20001

Name _____

Address_____

City, State, Zip Code_____

God the Black Man and Truth

Please enclose $15.00 plus $3.50 shipping & handling and mail to:

Communicators Press
P.O. Box 26063, Washington, D.C. 20001

Name _____

Address_____

City, State, Zip Code_____

God the Black Man and Truth

Please enclose $15.00 plus $3.50 shipping & handling and mail to:

Communicators Press
P.O. Box 26063, Washington, D.C. 20001

Communicators Press

To order other books by Communicators Press complete the order blank below and give the others to a friend or family member that they may further their understanding about God, His People and His Plan.

For more information or wholesale requests, write:

**Communicators Press, P.O. Box 26063
Washington, D.C. 20001**

Name _____
Address_____
City, State, Zip Code_____

The Impregnable People

Please enclose $17.00 plus $3.50 shipping & handling and mail to:

**Communicators Press
P.O. Box 26063, Washington, D.C. 20001**

Name _____
Address_____
City, State, Zip Code_____

The Impregnable People

Please enclose $17.00 plus $3.50 shipping & handling and mail to:

**Communicators Press
P.O. Box 26063, Washington, D.C. 20001**

Name _____
Address_____
City, State, Zip Code_____

The Impregnable People

Please enclose $17.00 plus $3.50 shipping & handling and mail to:

**Communicators Press
P.O. Box 26063, Washington, D.C. 20001**